A
COMMUNITY
OF
EXCELLENCE

Rich Harwood

ISBN: 1-4196-9390-5

ISBN-13: 9781419693908

INTRODUCTION

"You've known each other a long time, I'd guess?" asked the 70ish man standing at the end of the bar.

I turned and smiled broadly at his question. I had been thinking the exact same thing.

"Those two since I'm six, him since I'm seven." I answered, pointing first at Phil and Chris, then to Joe R.

The four of us had just spent a fabulous two and a half-hours in this small upstate bar one town over from Greenville New York. We were up there for a short four-day golf getaway. This was going to be our last night so we decided to spend it in the most neighborly kind of place we could find.

"It shows" He continued, nodding at his companion, also about 70. "We were just saying how we've been coming into this place for about 35 years and it's never been so good. You and your friends, well, we're just happy you stopped by. Thanks."

"So are we. You've got a real good group of people yourself."
I said.

"No. You don't understand." He was shaking his head, wearing an expression on his face that seemed far too serious for talking about hanging out in a bar. "Usually it's us two here. Those three over there. You see that big guy talking to Joe and Chris, he'll come in, get a beer and stand against the wall next to the jukebox all by himself. Not saying nothing to nobody. Have two, maybe three beers, give a couple of us a nod, and go. But you got him involved, singing, laughing and joking, just like everyone else. How do you do that?"

"Do what?" I asked confused.

"Just walk in here, not knowing a soul, and just get everyone going and partying like crazy. Aren't you worried you'll get tossed out on your ass?"

"No." I answered. "It never crossed my mind. We've been doing this for decades. It's really the only way we know. If you gonna go someplace new, you don't go and ignore whoever's there. Besides, this is a great place. I have a hard time believing what you said about everyone keeping to themselves. That's for real?"

"Sorry to say." The old man's friend chipped in. "This place never partied like this. Damnedest thing I ever saw. You guys really are special. Thanks for coming by."

"It's been our pleasure." I answered. Still not quite convinced. But there was no mistaking the look in their eyes. They were sincere in their gratitude and a touch saddened by the admissions they had just shared.

As I strolled back to Chris and Joe, I was thinking about what those two men had said. Are we special? Do we do things others don't? Are we really capable of converting a linebacker-sized wallflower into the man who was now smiling and joking with Chris and Joe? He looked up at me coming and winked. Chris, the two old men behind me and I, Joe couldn't see it, were all taken off guard until he turned to Joe and said. "You remind me of my roommate." Joe smiled. Putting his massive arm around Joe's shoulder, he continued "Yeah, just like my roommate when I was in prison."

Joe's reaction was priceless. As was the huge smile our new friend was broadcasting to everyone who turned at the sudden loud roar of laughter. I quickly turned to look back at the two men in the corner. They were doubled over with laughter, holding their sides with one hand and pointing at me and my friends with the other as if to declare, "Your Honor, I rest my case."

What just happened here? Could what they said be true? I was forced to go back in my mind over the day's events. We had a good round of golf, Phil and I actually playing golf, Chris and Joe found that it would be more fun for them to mess us up then to carve large divot holes in the grass. After piling back into my car, we then proceeded to head back to our motel about 15 minutes away. When I pulled up to the stop sign where I would have to turn right, we saw this bar across the street. We unanimously selected this place as a likely spot to end our week. I started feeling good vibes when a man indicated he was about to pull out of a parking spot right in front of the entrance. But, getting that spot required me to wait a couple of minutes for him to leave, so my friends went ahead to get things started. This meant that I was the last to enter. I could feel all eyes were on me as I approached the corner of the 'L' shaped bar, now staked out by Phil, Chris and Joe R, who were already outfitted with their beers. I could see the two old men in the corner to my left, a couple by the wall at the far end of the bar and a man with two young women about halfway down to Joe's right. The only other person there was the bartender.

"Is he the driver?" She asked. My three friends nodded at the attractive 25-year-old blond. "What will you have? He's buying." She said pointing at Phil.

"Him? Are you sure?" I asked confused. She nodded. "Then I'll need to see a menu."

"A menu?! In here? Are you nuts?!" She seemed a bit put off.

"Nuts, yeah probably." I explained. "But, its been 25 years since he's bought us a round and I want to make sure I get his money's worth."

The eight bystanders laughed just as hard as we did. Chris and Joe R were still laughing as I got my beer, but the ever-thrifty Phil was carefully counting his change. Joe took this opportunity to collect a dollar from everyone for the jukebox, making sure to ask the three female customers to come over and help pick out the songs. Even though they were about twenty years younger than him, all three felt comfortable enough to go right over with him and get some music going. From there the afternoon just seemed to take on a life of its own. People came. People intermingled. Sang together. Danced together. Laughed together. Got friendly. Anyone who walked in was invited by Joe's 'Staff" to chip in for the jukebox. Dues for the 'club', I guess. But, it did seem that the regular customers were now having a wonderful time together. And if what the two old men said was true, this was all very new to them. Thinking back, I suppose we did get it started.

But, does that make us special?

It didn't seem at all special to us. We really had been doing this for decades. It really is the only way we know. We learned it at a very early age. We learned it from our parents, older brothers and sisters, their friends, our neighbors. Almost everyone from our corner of the world, Flatbush, geographically the very center of Brooklyn, knew that the more people involved, whether it's a job or a party, the better off you were.

Inclusion is power. Exclusion is suicide.

The four of us had grown up in an environment that fostered community building. Being together. Supporting each other. Enjoying each other. Taking each other for who we each decided to be. Having fun together as a way of cementing that relationship and including as many newcomers into that fun as possible.

I wrote this book with the hope that it will explain that upbringing. Why we feel as we do. How we learned what we know. Who was there to show us the ropes. I wrote this book as the best way I know to explain to those two 70ish gentleman how we could just walk into a strange bar and get anyone feeling comfortable enough to join in and invite in others as well. I wrote this book to try and explain the ideals that were passed through Flatbush that led us to believe, feel and act as we do. I'll sometimes refer to these ideals as the "Code". I'd love to have a different word or phrase for the ideas and principles discussed, but this is the one we used, albeit rarely.

The explanation lies in how our community, our neighborhood, provided the five most important characteristics that allow any community, and each of its members, to feel comfortable enough and energized enough to thrive. To be great. To go forth and build on that greatness. To go forth and welcome new members to that community. To go forth and be excellent. We all understood that the benefits of being together, working together and celebrating together would make each of us an excellent person and allow all of us to build an excellent community.

Those five characteristics are security, courage, justice, tolerance and celebration. You must always cover your friend's back. Do the right thing, for yourself and for others. Work so that everyone gets what they earn. Encourage everyone to find their own path. Then get together to celebrate, reassure, and welcome.

I give each of these ideals a more specific definition than is common. I want each of them to be understood and appreciated for the influence they can have on a group of people when taken by themselves and in conjunction with the others. I have divided this book into sections that cover each characteristic, offering my definition and the benefits of each. Then followed by a series of stories that describe moments in my memories where I learned about it, saw it succeed or saw it fail.

The cumulative impact of these characteristics is excellence, again something that I have given a more limited definition than you are probably used to.

Excellence, in a community, is represented by the overall advance of that community's talents, energies, knowledge and innovation. Excellence is the motor of human advancement. It sits at the core of greatness, and at the core of happiness, and at the core of morality.

Excellence in the individual is the advancement of that person's feelings, beliefs, understanding, and contribution.

The key concept here is that no one can be excellent alone.

I am going to avoid digressing into a pseudo-philosophical treatise that justifies these beliefs. I will say this, though; we all want to be excellent at something. We all have an inborn need for acknowledgement, for success, and for praise. Plus, we all have the inborn ability to be excellent at something. Alas, we all also have the inborn weaknesses that stand in the way of that excellence. We need the strengths of others to help overcome our individual weaknesses. That is why no one can be excellent alone. That is why we congregate into communities with rules for interaction. We are better off for our neighbors' contributions. They are better off for ours. If we can focus that interaction to promote universal excellence, then we make a contribution to all the lives in that community.

In this book I will relate some of the events in my life that helped me learn about excellence. I start each part with a story featuring a member of my family who epitomizes the characteristic I am concentrating on. While we all worked to apply all the premises, the are a few individuals who stood a little taller when we consider the traits individually. I start each section with a family member in acknowledgement of them being our entry point, the beginning, the basis from which all else follows. Our family is our first community.

In my case, that included an intelligent, probing, powerful father and a sensitive, clingy, emotional mother. Eight distinctively different brothers and sisters, who personify the principles of loyalty, justice, courage, tolerance and celebration as well as any. But my family is more than this one household. Aunts, uncles, and cousins, both first and second, however many times removed, were also a strong influence on my life.

Both positive and negative.

Positive because of what they taught me and how they presented the lessons. Softball games and singalongs at the family picnics. Comic themes at our weddings, whether everyone was wearing sunglasses, outrageous hats, paper bags or Halloween masks. We expressed love and joy when we got together.

Negative because of the amusement they felt at my imaginary pets, wild stories, and vivid imagination. Traits of mine that became extremely evident at a very early age. Amusement that I misunderstood as ridicule. I was so sensitive to this perceived ridicule that I felt compelled to keep private from everyone my innermost thoughts and feelings. Hide them under the cover of brashness and noise. Prevent all from seeing my imagination and other talents to avoid the anticipated ridicule. It also compelled me to try and preempt the jokes by trying to be somebody that they thought I should be rather than who I thought I should be.

If you look at the cover photograph, you will see that I, second from the right, am slightly obscured. This is a very telling aspect of this picture. It signifies my attempts at the withdrawal that I just described. But that withdrawal was never complete. I still had to deal with the real world of my family and friends. To be successful at keeping these two worlds from colliding too drastically, I had to develop an ability to read circumstances and interpret whether it was safe to come out. This is the source of my overwhelming need to know why we do the things we do. Not to seek excellence using this knowledge but to hide from pain.

I seriously lacked the courage to do the right thing for myself. But this weakness of mine needed decades of exposure to my family and friends' strengths to finally stand aside. And it is from their strengths that I now have found the courage to identify that weakness and seek help from my community to overcome that sensitivity. This book is the result of that support from them. They could be counted on to do great things, be excellent examples of the Flatbush Principles, our Code.

This also goes for my first circle of friends. I always considered myself especially lucky to have had these five best friends that were part of my life from first grade until today. Steve, Phil, Chris, Joey D, me and Joe R, and a few others I could add to the list, and rightfully should, but it was the five people standing with me in the cover photograph that played the integral role of epitomizing the Flatbush principles I shared with you above. We love this picture. It captures our personalities and our togetherness while giving remarkable hints about how we interacted. One of those friends will be featured in the second story of each section.

Oh, about that man in the middle of the picture, sort of down in front. That's John, a coworker and former teacher of Phil's. But he could just as well have been the landlord, a gentleman we met in an upstate bar, or he could even be you.

He seems to be entering our circle. Joining in. Becoming part of the neighborhood, part of the community. He's welcome, as is anyone. Just step into that collective hug that seems to be extending from Chris' arms in the center. What makes John welcome? He's there and he looks like he's having fun. He's part of the party. He's included. He just needs to feel secure and make those around him feel secure too. He needs to have the courage to do the right thing. Be fair. And be tolerant. Share our idea that any are welcome.

In that same vein, I invite you to join us through this book.

Included are the events where I learned about doing the right things. About what it takes to feel comfortable enough to invite any and all to join in, any and all who would like to feel the camaraderie that I hope you see in those seven faces on the cover. I hope you see the power and wisdom in the ideals we'll be sharing. I hope you feel the warming, comforting joy when you see your community rise as one to right a wrong, step on injustice, or celebrate a success.

It would be great if we could help add an element to your life or your view of the world or to help you find your own road to excellence. But, all I really hope for is that you enjoy the book and agree we offer some thoughts that may help you feel a little better about things.

There will be quite a number of occasions in these stories when you will read about us drinking and going to bars. Yes, this was the forum for a lot of our celebrations but it was never just about the drinking. It was always about the company, the people you were with. Anywhere people gather you can have a community. The substance of these stories is the interaction of the people present and how that led to excellent things.

All the events you will read about in this book happened. More than likely, not exactly how I describe them. A memory wrapped in a flowing mane of gray hair and normal human filtering will have their say on the accuracy of the facts.

But these are my memories. Most are funny. Some a little sad. One is out and out tragic. But if I want those two elderly gentleman, and you, to understand the how, and why, of what we do, I can think of no better way than to share with you the incidents that impressed themselves on me to remind me about living up to being from Flatbush. And how special that really can be for anyone who seeks excellence, no matter where you are from. I hope I succeed

PART I - SECURITY

We learned early on about how important it is to 'cover your friends' backs'. To stay together so that all of us always feel that we had someone on our side when we stepped forward. To provide and be provided with security. Your friends have to know you can be relied on. You need to know they can be relied on. That no one has to face life's challenges and tests alone. Mess with one of us and you mess with all of us. There is nothing more powerful than a community rising up to show its members that any and all problems will be solved together. We are all in this together.

This doesn't mean we all have to go out and get German Shepherds and motion detection alarm systems. While having a sense of physical safety is vital, the most important part of this idea of security is that we make sure each community member thinks, believes and feels he or she is not alone. If we are going to feel energized enough to go out and be excellent we all need to know there are others close by to help whenever and in whatever way we need them. If you are in our community, then we'll help you overcome any failure and relish any success. If injustice is thrust your way, we will be next to you to fight it off. We humans exist on four levels; heart, soul, mind and body and it's in those portions that make up our souls where most of our advancement will come. It is the interior nature of our being where a sense of security will support excellence. If we possess a spiritual sense of connection to our neighbors than we can overcome all physical distances with our giving and receiving of support.

The stories that follow show both how a community can succeed and, unfortunately, fail in communicating the idea that we are all in this together. But even in failure the lessons learned about the security of our friends can be vivid and profound.

You Can't go off the Diving Board until You Swim the Pool

As I was growing up, I developed a reputation as a pretty good athlete. Hockey, Baseball, Football, not so much Basketball, but I could run faster than you'd think, jump higher than you'd think and I was stronger than I looked. Plus, I was very competitive.

That being said, I sucked at swimming. My sister Madeline could swim with the dolphins, I sank with the rocks.

So, as you could probably guess, I spent most of my summers between the ages of 6 and 12 at the pool. Not just any pool, Farragut Pool. A great place. The 'complex' had a bowling alley, cafeteria, paddle/hand ball courts, basketball, ping-pong, sunbathing, and a pool. A big pool. It was about 75 feet wide and 200 feet long. Shallow end, 1 and a half feet. Deep end, 8 feet. Two diving boards, 5 lifeguard seats. Two floating ropes. One between the toddler depth, 2 feet and less, and the other guarding the line over 4 feet. Three of the lifeguard chairs protected the deep end, and policed the diving boards.

To go off the diving boards, you had to swim in the deep end. To be allowed to swim in the deep end you had to swim the width of the pool while being watched by the lifeguards - and just about everyone else.

The swimming test process went as follows. The lifeguard would see you in the deep end, most likely going off one of the diving boards. If he felt that there was a question about your swimming ability, he would blow his whistle and wave you over, stand on his 6 foot high chair, blow his whistle to get the attention of the lifeguard on the other side of the pool 25 yards away, point straight down toward the top off your head, and wait for the other lifeguard to also stand on his chair and nod back he was ready.

He would then say: "Go ahead."

Or, you could volunteer by walking up to the lifeguard chair, climb onto the bottom step of the ladder, and ask to swim the pool.

I was 10 and must have prepared for my rite of passage for about 3 weeks. Practicing in the 3-foot level with some tutoring from three friends, Mike and the Woods brothers, who all swam on their school swimming teams. At first I was only able to get about half way before having to stand up. But I steadily gained more and more distance as the weeks of tutoring went on. Then, finally, after getting two thirds of the way across before standing, my friends told me that I was ready to step up to the lifeguard and volunteer for my test. I could do it now.

"But I didn't get all the way." I said.

They said that the deeper water held you up better, so it was easier to swim in 7 feet deep water than in 3 feet. Sounded reasonable. But, I think there was a chance that they were getting a little tired with dedicating a lot of fun time to wet-nursing me. Still, in spite of my verbal diploma, they added a warning. The most important thing was to swim the pool early in the morning. Less people making fewer waves. It's easier.

On the big day I got there at opening time, 8:00 AM. I met three of my friends at the door. We burst through the gate. The first thing you see, framed in the turnstile gate opening was the pool. And on that day, it looked gorgeous. A shimmering sheet of glass mirroring the crystal blue sky.

We ran to a table to drop off our towels and then to the 3-foot section to warm up. After a couple of minutes, my friends all went to the diving board. A little incentive, I guess. As I said, most of them were on their school's swimming team and were anxious to get back to the fun they used to have before I began my quest to swim the pool.

My warm-up lap complete, I was only about 5 feet away before I stood up, it was indeed time to do it. According to our plan, I was supposed to walk right up to the chair on the Albany Ave.

side of the pool. Step on the bottom rung and announce to the lifeguard, "I want to swim the pool."

Everything was set, the pool was practically empty because the surge of bathers had yet to arrive, but at this critical moment, I got scared. I froze. I was standing in the middle of the pool, in 3 and 1/2 feet of water, looking from my friends on the diving board to the lifeguard in that chair, to the rope that stood between me and the fun my friends were having. Board. Chair. Rope. Board. And then one of my friends waved me up. They all stopped diving to wave me an invitation to the deep end, to the diving board, to a new life that was one step closer to growing up.

In response to their cajoling, I moved. I waded strongly through the pool to the ladder, climbed strongly up the ladder steps, and strode strongly to the lifeguard chair and up onto the bottom step.

"I want to swim the pool." I declared strongly.

I was met with a welcoming big smile. "Okay kid."

The lifeguard stood up on his chair and sounded two quick whistle toots to alert his partner to the east that the procedure was about to begin. First, the finger point toward my head and the East guard waves his acknowledgement. I wave back and then change my expression from a smile to a determined grimace. I grit my teeth and dove right in.

The first part of a successful pool swimming strategy is to get as far across under water as you can. So I dove with all my might and pumped hard underwater until I had to take a breath. I broke the surface and started my stroke right away to keep up the momentum. I kept my head down and counted off the rhythm. Three strokes, three kicks, then turn my head to the left and take a breath. Head back down. Stroke. Kick. Concentrate on the stroke, the kicks, and the technique. If I can keep this tempo I'd be done in no time.

But I actually felt like I had been swimming for what seemed like two days.

"I must be almost done." I thought. Nope. About 2/3 of the pool to go. Keep going. Head down. Kick, kick, kick. Swing your arms. My stroke was very right-handed so I drifted to my left as I swam. This required me to take a look and correct my path at every breath.

So instead of a straight 25-yard juggernaut, I was more like slalom skier, saw-toothing my way over what was probably about 40 yards.

I was able to get a little more than halfway across before the doubts returned.

"Stop this diving board foolishness and get back behind the rope where you belong, idiot." I thought to myself. But I could hear my friends egging me on. The same friends who deserted me to go diving while I bobbed around in 3 feet of water. The same friends who had waved their invitation from the diving board. Loneliness plus foolishness is greater than self-doubt. I went on.

I went on until I did it. I can't remember, before or since, feeling anything like the triumph I felt as my hand scraped down on the concrete side of that pool. My maiden voyage at success. I did it. I had planned, practiced, sought out consultants, and overcame my fears, and now I get to walk with the big guys. Swim with the big fishes. This felt very much like 'Today I am a man!'

When I finally arrived at the far end, I was right where that infernal rope met the side of the pool. About 25 feet left of the direct line that should have landed me at the foot of the eastside lifeguard chair. The lifeguard had climbed down and walked to the point where I landed and helped me up from the pool. He probably did this to be closer to me in case I went under. But I thought he was welcoming me to a new life as a bigger, successful human being - almost a man.

A grand gesture of esteem.

"Good job. Congratulations." he said.

His name was John. He was maybe 18 years old. And just then he became my newest hero. The first thing I saw when I achieved my first big accomplishment was John's smiling face behind a hand extended to assist me out of the water. Before now, he was the law. The whistle that yelled at me to stop running, no splashing, no rough housing, get back BEHIND THE ROPE. But not anymore. My sister Madelyn was wrong. He was great. He was my friend, my hero.

"Thanks." I sputtered.

My wheezing, gasping body was sitting on the side of the pool, recovering. The 15 or 20 people who were watching mostly were drifting away, though some said nice things and "Good job" and stuff like that. It was a good three-minute show for them. The kid made it. And it was one of the Harwoods, Tommy's and Madelyn's little brother.

I had to move. So I got up and walked, no I strutted, over to the water fountain. Not because I was thirsty, but more because it was next to the diving board. This way I could be cool and still get right over to the prize. My first dive off the diving board. The first rite of passage in a ten-year-old's mind. Swimming the pool was just the road to travel to the diving board Holy Grail.

The line for the 'A' board was only about four people long. Three of who were my friends and swimming consultants, the two Woods brothers and Mike. They were real happy to see me but there was little celebration because our time on the 'A' board was precious. Even though it was still early, not even 10:00 AM, we had to get our time in on the good board before the older and good divers came and took it over. Once Lucky or the other really good divers got there, the kids, out of respect, went to the less springy board on the Albany Ave side of the pool. The path least traveled by admiring girls.

Mike's older brother, Billy, was one of those good divers. He arrived just then and got on line right in front of us. This was not cutting, but our signal to move over to the other board. I took this opportunity for a quick detour into the locker room right behind us to go to the bathroom.

By the time I got back, there were about 7 good divers going on board A, and maybe a dozen kids on board B. I stood between the two boards and watched the good divers for a couple of minutes until one of my friends just finished a dive and got to the back of the line. I got on line behind him.

Life was great. I had made it. On line with my friends to go off the diving board. Lucky and his compatriots casually competing on the 'A' board. A few dozen people watching them. Only my best lifeguard friend John watching us as he had rotated to the near chair. I had swum the pool, I had grown up a little and I was in paradise.

My turn. I strode proudly to the end of the board and hopped with all my might. The board did not.

I weighed maybe 50 pounds and probably looked more like 8 years old when I was 10. I hopped again, but the board's indifference continued. So I conceded to the inevitable and just dove. Very conservative. Not one of our favored splash producers: no cannonball, no can-opener, not even a cassaza (high jump, land in a sitting position). Even though my friends were in the midst of competing to see who could make the biggest splash, I just offered a simple hands overhead straight in dive. I even angled it toward the ladder to make it easier on myself. "Don't get greedy. Take your time. You've got your whole life ahead of you to get into the funky dives." I thought to myself.

Splash, surface, stroke, kick, kick, kick, stroke, grab the ladder. Pull myself up.

Whistle.

Everyone stopped.

My hero, John was calling me.

Why? He had cleared me to dive not a half-hour ago. Maybe he wants to tell me how good I looked. Maybe give me a diving pointer.

I walked to the foot of the chair.

"You have to SWIM THE POOL, KID."

CRASH! BURN! SLAM!

"What?!" I said. "I just swam the pool before! You pulled me out! You said I did great!"

"That's tough kid. You can't go off the diving board until you swim the pool."

I was devastated. Really more confused than angry.

This was my first experience with injustice out in the cold, cruel world. This was very different from my brother taking a larger share of the can of soda we were splitting. Very different from my younger brother staying up later than me and getting to watch 'I Spy'. This was my hero betraying me!!

"But John?,... I "

"You can't go off the diving board until you swim the pool."

"But.."

"You can't go off the diving board until you swim the pool."

Madelyn was right. He was the worst. I should have realized that a 13-year girl does far more research and has far more insight into the qualities of the lifeguards than I had. I looked up. He was ignoring me. Only responding to my voice with a curt, robotic repetition of the rule.

My friends were back on line trying to be invisible. They wouldn't back me against John. He would make all off us swim the pool.

I was alone.

I was despondent. Crushed. Crestfallen. I was scared. Scared that this time I wouldn't make it. All the progress, the growing, the steps toward manhood were gone. I would be stepped on. I would be shunned. I could sense my whole world coming to an end.

"Okay." I said feebly.

John stood up as I walked around the chair to be clear of the chain that fenced off the pool end around the diving boards. He was whistling to the other lifeguard. Every sound in that pool stopped. In the time since I last swam the pool, Farragut Pool had gotten a lot busier. Activities were in full swing. But they all paused because they heard the whistle and saw the lifeguards stand on their chairs.

The older divers stopped. The kid divers stopped. Courtesy demanded it. Diving chopped the water. The 25 or so diving spectators had only one thing to watch. Me.

The word spread. "John was making Little Harwood swim the pool again and he just did it this morning."

Fifteen people got up from the round steps to watch. The water fountain line stopped drinking to watch. The people going into or out of the locker room stopped to watch. The 75 people wading on the other side of the rope stopped to watch. Mah jongg games were suspended. Paddleball players took a time out. Everyone and everything stopped. Everyone and everything was focused on one thing, me.

"Go ahead kid."

If I was 4 or 5 years older I'd have called him a bastard, but that was not in the code for a 10-year-old kid. I looked at the other side. No smile this time. No wave. Just a lot of water. A LOT of water. Miles of water.

"We ain't got all day kid. Now or get on the other side of the rope."

I dove in. My concentration was jumping all over the place. Stroke, kick, kick, kick. This is wrong. He just saw me swim the pool. Kick, kick, kick. How close am I. Don't go left. Aim for the ladder. He's really unfair. How am I ever going to make it this time?

I changed my stroke technique for this lap. Instead of keeping my head down for three strokes then turn to the side for a breath, I kept it up over the surface. This was more work, but I could see where I was going and went straighter than before.

I had a good flow going now. I had succeeded in focusing my concentration away from the distractions and zeroed in on the steps of the ladder as my goal. A small hint of a self-satisfied gloat began to spread from my heart as I saw the ladder approaching and realized that I had plenty of strength left to get there. About 6 feet from the ladder, a chop in the water passed me, hit the wall and splashed back in my face. The kid divers had also reasoned that I had made it and resumed the splash contest. But, that splashing ruined me. I swallowed some water. Gagged. Choked. Coughed.

SPLASH.

The other lifeguard, I don't remember his name, dove in when he saw me gag. I was startled. I stopped swimming. He grabbed me.

"You okay kid?"
"What are you doing? I'm fine. I just swallowed some water."
"You looked like you were going down."
"But I'm fine! I swam the pool, right?"

He looked over at John. He gave me the thumbs down.

"Sorry kid. No. You didn't make it. You have to get on the other side of the rope."

"But I made it. You didn't have to help me. I was right there."

"Sorry kid."

The tears started. "But I made it."

"Sorry kid. Let's go."

I climbed out of the pool. Shouldered my way through the dozens of silent onlookers. Stomped my way toward the stairs. Then I ran. I ran soaking wet, barefoot, over the concrete into the backcourt the exact opposite direction from my towel. The backcourt was an area usually shunned because it had more rocks on the surface that really hurt your feet. But right then I didn't notice. The pain in my heart was drowning out any physical pain at that moment. I was crying. I was running. I ran to the very back of the secondary handball courts and behind the hedges the lined the three story fence on the Forty-second St. side of the complex. The corner closest to Glenwood Road.

I wailed and bemoaned the injustice. I decried the humiliation of a lifeguard jumping in to help me when I didn't need him. I was a pitiful kid hiding because I had just had my first bubble of naiveté popped. I felt powerless and overwhelmed.

This is when we need to rely on our family and friends to bail us out.

This became my sister Madelyn's finest hour. She came to get me.

Madelyn was then and still is a great lady. She had a social standing in the pool because she was one of St. Vinnie's Swim Team's best swimmers. At a pool like this those were the kids that provided leadership to their crowds. But here athletic ability was only the tip of her social iceberg. She was also known for sticking by her family and friends through thick and thin. Her friends knew that if anyone dared to give them any grief that Madelyn would be standing right at their shoulder to make sure the were covered.

Plus, she and I always got along well. In the political arena that exists in every household I could be counted on not to instantly take the 'male' side in disputes. My older brothers, Tommy and Bobby, would occasionally team up in some 'he said/she said' argument. But, even if my voice held the least weight, I usually stayed neutral or even defended Madelyn. Later on she would get me my first job at Bohack's Supermarket.

But there was something else. Something else Madelyn and I had in common. We both had the very un-Harwood like ability to get nasty. I'm not talking about angry. I'm talking about nasty. When we lose our tempers, our pulse will slow down. We will get quiet. We can think clearly. We can get mean. We will act. And Madelyn was very clear about what had to be done.

John had pissed her off. She hadn't seen what happened but word spread real fast. The general consensus was the John was a bastard. He really screwed a little kid. Some of Madelyn's friends had seen it. Saw me run. Two of them were with her when she found me finally coming out of the hedge, all cried out. Sheepishly resigned to going back in the pool on the other side of the ropes.

But Madelyn had a different plan. She had decided that John could not be allowed to get away with doing this to someone. Not to anyone, and definitely not to her little brother.

She told me that when John got down from his chair to go on break, the other lifeguard, the one who had jumped in to save me, would let me swim the pool, again, but without the whistle and the show.

Great! I cheered up immediately. I started capering around like a puppy. That energy must have carried over because I did indeed succeed this time. Without a problem, even through the choppy water. Kept the stroke. I even went straight.

The fact that injustice exists in the world means we can never sleep. We can never allow it to win out. We can't slink to the other side of the rope when we see it. After we have cried, whined, bemoaned, wailed, and cursed. After we have gotten pissed off, we need to find support from family and friends and go back and face it, again and again confident in the fact that our community is there with us.

My community had very clearly stood taller than the transgressions of John the Lifeguard that day. His attempts to use his authority and power to suppress was no match for my family and friends who decided that I should get another chance to succeed. I passed a milestone, I swam the pool and moved to a new level of excellence, because my sister and her friends wouldn't settle for anything less.

IT'S FRIGGAN' RICHIE

Take a second and look at the picture on the cover. Focus on the guy third from the left, sort of in the middle. That's Chris; big, loyal, hearty Chris. You're not mistaken if you get the idea that he's trying to bear hug us all. Chris isn't interested in the existentialist theory of life or why we're here on earth. To him, life is about taking care of those closest to you, he knows that you keep family and friends as close as you can and you stick by them no matter what. If you ever found yourself in the midst of any kind of confrontation that might escalate into a fight, in merely seconds you'd find Chris right beside your shoulder. No friend of his would ever have to deal with a problem alone.

One very fine illustration of this came after Chris had started work at his first corporate job selling office equipment. He worked for a huge company that manufactured its own products, which were distributed by an in-house sales force. Chris spent his first two years selling upstate and then finally worked a transfer back to a territory back home in the New York area. He could now take care of some of his people. New Yorkers.

As expected Chris spent the first few weeks with his new territory getting to know his customers. Visit after visit. Person by person. Introducing himself and his products. Getting to know the people he would be taking care of and their needs. But, unlike other salesmen who use like terms, to Chris this meant that he needed to find out what he could do for them. How he needed to cover their backs so that they could be successful. He understood to his very marrow that his own success must grow from the success of the people he took care of.

One day his manager announced a corporate pricing change that had to be rolled out almost immediately. The suits at HQ included a special incentive bonus that struck a particularly excitable nerve in the manager. He decided that all his salespeople were going to contribute to his winning this incentive. The manager had taken the liberty of identifying those customers that he was going to personally visit to induce the purchases that would lead to his reward. Chris felt very upset about this. "This manager was not going to force something down MY clients throats. Not if I can do something about it." But this response bothered Chris too. He felt the same kind of loyalty to his company. He worked out a great solution. He covertly called one of those clients. The one he had made a deep connection with almost immediately. They talked and figured out a strategy that could help both sides of this equation.

Chris made sure to schedule his new friend's place as their first stop on the day he was to accompany his manager on their trip to

Chris' customers. The actual conversation would be directed to the friend's mother who ran the equipment wholesaler. Their strategy worked out very well. The manager was able to get some of the extra activity he lusted for but Chris' client did ok by the deal too. Chris then translated the success at the first meeting to the strategy he and the manager would use for the rest of that day's calls. Success all around.

Chris was never the most eloquent of us. But he did give an excellent lesson in this kind of camaraderie and loyalty to one of Phil's younger brothers, Andrew, one night outside Mahoney's, our home bar.

There was a fight. It involved a good friend of ours, Jimmy, who was squaring off with the ex-boyfriend of Jimmy's current girlfriend, and future wife. This was the fifth time in a series of seven fights between these two. All seven occurring within a three-month period. We had all become real tired of the fights after their second rematch.

To stop these fools from interrupting our party once again, four of Jimmy's childhood friends and I starting pushing him from friend to friend to try and bounce the rage out of him. This would tire him out and prevent him from getting near his foe who was pinned against a door about 25 ft away. Judging that the exercise we put Jimmy through had cooled him off enough, we let him go over and have his say. Chris saw this and he got right over to Jimmy and put him in that bear hug of his to keep his friend safe.

I heard Mooney's voice say, "You better get Chris off him before he gets hot again." Mooney's words represented the consensus of Jimmy's childhood friends behind me. So I got a hold of Chris to pull him away, Joe R quickly coming in to help me with the much bigger friend. Our struggle spun us around and we three landed in a pile on the hood of a parked car. Joe R broke off and allowed me to wrestle with Chris as he calmed down. Andrew, about Chris' size, jumped to my defense. He stepped in and grabbed Chris by the head to pull him off of me. Fearing Chris would explode before he realized who had grabbed him, Joe R and I jumped in fast and succeeded in placing ourselves between them. We walked Chris away, telling Andy not to move and to calm down.

Of all of Phil's brothers, Andy had been the one who latched on to us the closest. He had grown up watching his three older brothers develop good strong friendships with my older brothers and me. Andy looked up to his older brothers so much that he felt a strong kinship to his brothers' first circle of friends. But because he was just a year or two younger than us, he picked Phil and me over Tommy's and Peter's friends to get closer to.

Phil's contingent of close friends grew when Chris and Joey D and then Steve, Danny and finally Joe R joined in. We had become a very close-knit group about seven years before this fight but our friendship dated back at least eight years before that. Andy had watched us together on many occasions and saw the quiet, deep comfort we felt in each other's company. He saw the clear enjoyment we had at each other's expense without losing respect for each other's individuality. He had the pleasure of witnessing a couple of our card games, which were less about gambling and more about togetherness. It looked like money we were throwing in the pot but you would know it wasn't about money when the winner of $40 would lend the loser of five, $10 for our apres-cards party at Mahoney's. Our card games meant that Chris would stink up the room with one of those cigars. That Phil would fail for the sixth year in a row to get those same ten pennies into the pot. That Joe R would create a new game, which he always seemed to win. That fat lips would be made fun of, that 'thriftiness' would be complained about and that the seven-second alarm clock would go off when I wouldn't shut up. It was only natural that Andy would get worried that there might have been cracks in our rock-solid friendship when he saw Chris and I wrestling. So, he acted, even though he was mistaken about the cracks.

After another fifteen minutes or so, everything now calm, I left Chris to talk to Jimmy and then went back into the bar to find Joe R explaining to Andy why we had jumped up to stop him from defending me against Chris. Not a minute later, Chris pushed past me to get right into Andy's face.

Chris begins his lecture with a paternal expression that clearly showed the mixture of anger and compassion that Chris felt. With a raised finger under Andy's nose he shouts, "Don't ever grab me like that! I'm telling you, if you weren't Phil's brother I'd mash you right now."

"But it was friggan' Richie?!!" pleaded Andrew.

"That's the whole point.' Countered Chris. "I'm not gonna hurt Richie and he's not gonna hurt me. We couldn't. Phil, me, Richie, Steve, Joe, you'd never see one of us go after another. Didn't you see Joe walk away?" Chris asked.

"Yeah." Said Andy.

"Don't ya think he knows better than you? He wasn't worried. You know Joe's not going to lose my back, or Richie's. He knows we're not gonna fight. Especially not over this stupid spit. It's just like when you fight with your brothers, we ain't gonna hurt each other we're covering each others' backs. And we're not gonna lose your back either because your Phil's brother."

Pure and clear and simple. No one is alone.

THE NUNS — PART 1

Not counting my two-week career as a kindergartner, I started school in September, 1962. The school in question was St. Vincent Ferrer, located on the corner of Glenwood Road and East 37th Street, a mere three quarters of a block from my house.

My memories of first grade are pretty much gone, though I do remember being the smallest boy in the class, third smallest overall. This was easy to determine because back then the normal order of things went by height. Smallest up front, tallest behind. The first rating system I was confronted with had me feeling small, low, and insignificant.

My other memory from that year was, understandably, of my teacher, Sr. Winifred. She seemed a giant among women. Standing almost 5 feet tall. With one of the warmest, most welcoming, cheery smiles God has ever blessed this Earth with. Rightfully he surrounded it with the roundest, shiniest, rosiest cheeks you could ever imagine. Beautifully enhanced by the wimple frame that Dominican Sisters wore at that time. Soft spoken and cheerful she was the quintessential first grade teacher, and everything you could ever expect a nun to be. Who, by and large, were very dedicated and deeply committed to God and their education responsibilities.

The education of most of the participants in these stories was entrusted to nuns, of many different orders. At St. Vincent Ferrer, we had Dominican Nuns. Kentucky Dominicans. I'm sorry to say that there were some Sisters who did not live up to their calling as well as Sr. Winifred. Albeit a minority, some of the nuns were less interested in the inspiration of their students to find their road to excellence and more interested in preventing their souls from burning in hell.

But, by and large, they were wonderful people who had dedicated their lives to God and Church. Traditionally they could expect one of two careers, nurse or teacher. In our school, Sr. Winifred, Sr. Mary Alice, the music teacher, and Sr. Brendan, the principal, were natural educators who worked very well with us kids. The rest, though possessed with sincere intentions and pure hearts, did not have the same talent and fell a certain distance shy of being good teachers. Regardless of the results of their efforts, I will always give them the credit that that type of lifelong commitment and soulful purity deserves. Most had wonderful hearts, even if the talent wasn't there.

But there were some of them that never should have been teachers. And, regretfully, I had my share of these.

This community that was Flatbush - a community that went to great lengths to show, explain, and emulate the qualities of excellence - allowed an under-qualified, though well intentioned, group of people, to teach the future members of that community. This flawed approach ignored the divine mission of excellence, and instead sought to instill them with a fear of God, sin, and eternal damnation as a priority over an excitement for learning. It's not the nun's fault that this ideal went awry, but their role in the failing of our schools was prominent, because of the fiduciary responsibility that was thrust on them. A better thought out system of educating the youth of a community is to allow action, thought, and imagination to awaken the children's thirst for knowledge. Expose them to seek out any and all areas of inspiration. Then allow them to experiment with the information, their interpretation, and the results of their activities. Feedback being supportive, informative, and enlightening. Already saddled with a poorly conceived education system, the Sisters cannot be held responsible for the shortfall of the results. But they can be held responsible, individually, for their own personal failings.

The three stories that follow, all including my seventh grade teachers, give three instances where the Dominican Sisters failed in their role as nurturers of the next generation of excellent citizens of Flatbush. One worked out okay, but the other two stories are about the nuns failing as Sisters, failing as Catholics, failing as Christians, failing as teachers, and failing as people.

Roman Catholic education in the 1960's was very different from the education my children receive today. For one thing, corporal punishment was not only accepted, it was expected. Too much time was spent showing us what couldn't and shouldn't be done rather than trying to help us tap into our special talents and seeing a healthy way to express ourselves. Also the feedback centered on our limitations. Kids were divided according to 'brains'. The smartest in Group I, the mediocre in Group II, the challenged in Group III. The criteria for these classifications were very arbitrary and almost always 'permanent'. I only remember one occasion when someone was promoted from Group II to Group I during my eight years at St. Vinnies. Of the six faces in the cover photograph, 4 were in Group III, including the two who are the most financially successful today. Joe D, the brilliant engineer, was in Group II. I was in Group I.

Almost as bothersome to me was that we had one teacher for every subject while we were in grades 1–5. In sixth, you watched as the teachers rotated from room to room to teach a specialty.

In seventh grade, the school decided to experiment a little. The students were to rotate from class to class. Plus, to their credit, they decided to discontinue the segregation of the three groups and intermingled us in the different classes. They must have believed that this approach would be a better preparation for high school.

But, the changing of classes had to be done with appropriate Dominican decorum. Only carry the books for the next two classes. No talking. Measured, deliberate pace. Eyes straight forward. Stay against the wall. Only cross the hall at right angles and only after passing the doors of the outlying classrooms. Actually, with about a 155 students divided into three classes, this discipline was probably indispensable. We hated it anyway.

The three nuns we had in seventh grade were Sr. Appeline, who taught History and Geography, Sr. Helen Marie, English and Religion, and Sr. Pauline, Math and Science.

My Group I status notwithstanding, I wasn't a good student. I wouldn't do my homework, I wouldn't study and I wouldn't read. But, I still got 90's so no one seemed to notice.

No one except Sr. Pauline.

Actually I feel compelled to refer to her as Sr. Marlita. That was her name when I had her in 3rd grade. Which was before I came to the ill-founded conclusion that I would be better off dumbing down to avoid the ridicule I expected from my friends. I worked very hard at not being smart. Sr. Marlita was the one who saw through the act.

"If only this child would read. He could be the smartest kid in the class." She told my mother on many occasions.

While reading in of itself wasn't that bad, there was no way I was going to do anything to be the smartest in my class. She got pretty frustrated about this. Not only was this wasting my talents, it seemed to her some kind of sin. I should use God's gift for good, not to be a quick mouthed wise guy.

This frustration culminated in an explosion on her part that grew into an incident that fed off the already strained relationship I had with my classmates. But it allowed her, and others, to show me lessons in dignity, class, and, especially, justice.

The fuse for this episode was stomping up the stairs.

Our 7th grade class was located in the old school building, occupying two floors above the church. For some forgotten reason we had to go to the new school building located over the Auditorium across 37th St. On the way up, I heard some wise guy classmates behind me stomping in cadence up the stairs.

I, as usual, was up in the front of the line. (Remember, we used height order for just about everything.) If there was going to be some wising off, I had to be a part of it. So I picked up the cadence. Sr. Marlita freaked. She stopped the line and hustled to the rear to apprehend the guilty parties.

And guess whose was the first face she saw. Mine.

"Mr. Harwood, because of your immaturity, this entire class will have to come back to school tomorrow for one hour." She screamed.

Now, in my defense, I was about to mention that I had only stomped the last three or four steps while others in line had been stomping for two flights. But she cut me off. She wasn't finished.

"And Mr. Harwood, I hope they beat you for this."

I was shocked. My mouth dropped open. Did she really say that? Yes, those were her words.

I knew I was dead. Didn't she realize that there were guys out there who were licking their chops for a good reason to take a shot at the wiseass shrimp who always seemed to be on a mission to convince the world he knew everything.

Oh boy, was I dead.

The next morning, Wednesday, I woke up sick. Assuredly anxiety. But I convinced my mother this was real. It was a pretty common ritual for me to fake sickness to try and stay home from school. On rare occasions, I succeeded. And this was definitely a day I needed to stay home. She succumbed, so I spent that day lying on the couch forgetting my troubles as I watched TV.

However, at about 12:30, I repented. I told my mother about the staying after. How it was kind of my fault that we had to go back at 2:00 pm for an hour. (On Wednesdays the school got out at 1:00 pm). I suggested that I was duty bound to go, since I was now feeling better. She agreed and I got on the uniform and started the walk to school.

By the time I got to the corner I was sick again.

I got as far as the schoolyard gate. They were waiting. They said that I should be beaten, just as Sister said. And they rushed me.

Not a happy moment.

8 – 12 kids took off after me.

Now I needed to outrun them for that three quarters of a block to my house. Luckily for me, the only kid in class fast enough to have a chance to catch me decided that he would sit out this particular beating.

I got home safely. The last angry young man giving up about three houses from mine.

The ensuing conversation with my mother was not a good one. But it turned out better than I expected.

I told her everything that had transpired. The stomping. The screaming. The three steps vs. two flights. The 'hope they beat you' edict. The threats. The chase. I was expecting her to side with the nuns. Something like, 'She would only say that if you deserved it.' That's what parents did then. Nuns, brothers and, especially, priests were religious devotees, servants of God. Right as right can be.

Except this time, my mother decided that they were wrong.

Sr. Marlita was wrong.

And my mother decided she was going to make it right. She was going to take care of this herself. Do the right thing. Right now.

She took me by the hand and we marched right out the door up the block to the Convent entrance on 38th Street. No one answered. We walked into the schoolyard to a school entrance. Locked. As a last resort we went to the Rectory. We waited there while the secretary made numerous calls to the Convent before she found out that the nuns had been in the Chapel before, but Sr. Brendan would be available now. So we marched the two short blocks back to the Convent.

Sr. Brendan answered the door herself. She and my mother went into her office and they left me alone in the waiting room. A few minutes later, Sr. Brendan left her office, passed by the waiting room, and returned a couple of minutes later with Sr. Marlita.

Next, she came to get me.

"Well young man," Sr. Brendan started. "What a fine little mess we have. Your mother is upset. Sister is upset. And I'm upset. You understand what you did?"

"Yes Sister, that's why I told my mother that I should go back to school to stay after." I replied.

"He did do that." My mother confirmed.

"That's very like him." Supported Sr. Marlita

"Okay then. But what are we to do about your classmates?" Sr. Brendan continued.

"I should be the one to take care of that, Sister. It's my fault they acted as they did." Offered Sr. Marlita.

Okay. Then the only thing left is for me to tell the parents of the children who chased you." Said Sr. Brendan.

My mind screamed, 'You can't do that. They'll really kill me then' though no sound came out of my mouth. My face must have divulged this terror because Sr. Brendan asked,

"Would you rather I not tell them?"

"Yes Sister."

"What if they come after you again? We can't have that." She asked.

"I don't know. I'm faster than them. And Sr. Marlita said she'd tell them not to." I pleaded.

Sr. Brendan gave and got nods from the other adults in the room. When she turned her face to me, I got that kind-hearted look in her eye very clearly as she said, "Okay, so we are all agreed. Sister will talk to the class and make sure they understand. Your behavior will improve drastically so we have no repeats of this episode. But, remember, we expect that not only your behavior will improve but your studies as well. Nothing would make the three of us happier than for you to stop the wising around and concentrate on your studies." I nodded my agreement.

The meeting was adjourned with some good things on that twelve year old mind. I knew now that I didn't have to face my problems alone. My back was covered from then on.

THE NUNS — PART 2

The next event in this Sisterly saga also took place in the seventh grade. This story however is not quite as uplifting.

My homeroom, English and Religion teacher was Sr. Helen Marie. Four feet and ten inches of New England righteousness and about 100 pounds of fury.

"Get the YAD stick" was how she would pronounce someone's doom. This greatest of the supporters of the corporal punishment expectations in school was also the only nun since third or fourth grade who used the stick on the girls as well as the boys.

Punishment from her was swiftly, furiously, and very energetically administered. The condemned party was put on public display for their requisite humiliation whether that party was guilty or not. Our little Torquemonde rarely felt the need for investigation.

Sr. Helen Marie became infamous for two conspicuous actions, though two different segments of the community each focused on a different one.

The first was as appalling an action as a hard working Catholic parent in 1969 could imagine from a seventh grade teacher, especially the Religion teacher. She read a copy of Playboy Magazine in Religion class. You read correctly. Bunny head, centerfold, risqué comics. WE didn't read it. She did. But we watched her do it. Right at her desk, right in the front of the class with both boys and girls witnessing. She even unfolded the centerfold for the full view.

Being short and relegated to one of the front seats, I got a ringside seat to this lesson in maturity, which is what she called it. A lesson to show us that sexuality, though she never mentioned that word, is not a sin.

I actually thought she had a point, when I gave it a little more consideration. Her point? A magazine can't commit a sin, only people can. So, if you read the magazine as a 'Young Christian Teenager', with maturity and reflection, then you were not sinning. If you deal with sex as a conscientious 'Young Christian Teenager' then you're not committing a sin. This did seem a bit reasonable.

The parents, however, disagreed. Big time.

I don't remember if any ramifications befell Sr. Helen Marie for this transgression, but I do recall the Pastor and Principal having to meet with quite a number of parents and some note was sent home. But for all this uproar, she stayed with us right to the end of the term.

And it was a torturous end.

She was so obsessed with this idea of us becoming 'Young Christian Teenagers' that we spent every Religion class focussing on what she believed that responsibility entailed. Boring you may say, but not particularly torturous.

True enough. Until she committed that second infamous action. Until she found us an anthem.

"I Gotta Be Me" by Sammy Davis Jr.

Not a bad song, really. But we had to listen to it repeatedly, over and over again, writing the lyrics on the side black board, making changes as they were uncovered, all afternoon, every afternoon. For the last two months of the year.

Those lyrics never left that board. I saw them in English class. I saw them in Religion class. I saw them to start the day. And I saw them to end every day. I doubt that any member of my class would have any trouble singing along, albeit subconsciously, if we ever heard that song again. But, in my case, God has been a merciful God and I haven't heard it for decades. If I had, I'm not sure if I weren't singing along subconsciously I'd be screaming the lyrics all the way to the nearest psych hospital.

Now that you have a pretty decent idea of what Sr. Helen Marie was capable of, I want to share the penultimate incident in my memory that establishes a serious psychosis on her part. I hope it was a mental health problem. If she couldn't defend herself by declaring insanity, then I would have to classify her as one of the most evil people I have ever met. Not the kind of endorsement a Dominican Sister should have.

Sr. Helen Marie had the boys lined up in alphabetical order, not height, along the front blackboard to turn in an essay assignment for English. She wanted to spend a few moments to review them with us, personally. She started with Cassazza; I was about seventh on line, behind a kid named Foley.

Foley and the kid in front of him were acting up in line. Fay was talking, probably telling some joke, because Foley was squeaking and snorting poorly stifled laughter. I wish he had been quieter.

In only a matter of seconds, Mount Sister Helen Marie erupted.

She bolted from her chair, left hand unsheathing her sword of a YADstick. Leaping in a most Samurai fashion, she landed the perfect distance to my left and unleashed her best Ted Williams (New England girl, remember) two-hand, dead pull, home run swing. This huge, arching swipe landed flush on Foley's cheek as he turned to see what that movement was next to him. While he didn't see the YADstick coming, he did see an expression on her face that would have stopped a Beserker dead in his tracks.

She landed a perfect strike. A strike that could have floored a bull elephant and ordinarily would have floored Foley, except that it had been slightly deflected.

By my face.

The metallic end of the half-inch thick stick had sliced through my face right under my left eye. Along the line of the bottom edge of the eye socket. Less than a quarter inch below the eye. A quarter of an inch below blinding me.

The blood started flowing instantly. This blood flow distracted her. It succeeded in slowing her down. But it didn't stop her.

The tirade for Foley that would normally have accompanied the blow was instead replaced with the following statement:

"Mr. Harwood, I know you didn't do anything, but you can consider that a down payment on the next time you get it."

She then went back to her seat.

I was struck paralyzed. I didn't know what to do. I was even afraid to wipe the quickly flowing blood so as not to provoke her any further. It ran down my cheek and neck until meeting the collar of my shirt and spreading along its edge from nape to tie knot. It took the girls in their seats making gross out noises and asking Sister to take care of the blood flow before she would stop reviewing essays and attend to my cut.

I was finally given a Band-Aid obtained from one of the other teachers. Sr. Helen Marie didn't even show a second of concern or remorse.

If a community's education system is expected to uphold the ideals that community wants its citizens to follow, then this Nun failed miserably in her responsibilities. How insecure does a kid need to feel if he is intimidated to the point where he won't even wipe blood off his face for fear of further punishment? How can a child find the courage to do the right thing if he has no courage to do anything? What kind of justice is it when the good kid gets the bloody face? What kind of example of tolerance is it to be intimidated by a tortured soul imposing a definition of what a conscientious teenager should be? An imposed definition of proper sexuality? An imposed definition of what each of us was to do, to be, and, what's worst, what to think. And she didn't even have the wherewithal to admit a mistake or apologize.

We weren't in this together. Sr. Helen Marie was more concerned about fulfilling some deviant internal influence than trying to prepare her students for their futures, whether they followed a path of a young Christian teenager or not. "Scare the devil out of them and they can't do evil" was the mantra that governed her educational activities. The fact that she was doing evil things to "scare" us into being young Christian teenagers never seemed to bother her.

But still there was worse to come.

THE NUNS — PART 3

I called the previous story the penultimate event in Sr. Helen Marie's career at St. Vinnies. This next incident took place very near to the end of the term. And it included the third of the Nuns teaching my seventh grade class. Actually, she precipitated it.

She was Sr. Appeline.

She had an altogether different personality as Sr. Helen Marie. As demonstrative as Sr. Helen Marie was, that's how stiff Sr. Appeline was. She had a high pitched, nasal drone of a voice. She was as good a caricature of an anal-retentive, anti-social nerd as you could stuff into a Nun's habit. Though in her case, five foot two and as thin as a rail, it wouldn't be too tough a stuff.

But don't let that quiet, nerdy, 90-pound weakling thing fool you. She was just as big a psycho as was Sr. Helen Marie. And they teamed up to commit the most vicious, atrocious act of violence I have ever witnessed anywhere and at any time in my life before or since.

Sr. Appeline had a very different way of teaching from what we were used to. I think that to compensate for her lack of a voice, she would circle around the class as she taught, droning on about that day's History or Geography lesson. Occasionally, and usually without making eye contact, she would verify students' attentiveness by sneaking a question into her dirge which was quickly followed by a squeaking of someone's last name.

And, don't be her target and not have the answer. For then she would repeat what she had been droning about thereby making your classmates hate you.

But, it was even worse if you were talking or fooling around. The woman had to have had eyes in the back, both sides and under her head because no one ever got away with anything in her class. Surprising when you consider the thick pointy frame glasses that she wore.

Danny found out about that.

Danny could have been the seventh face in our cover photo. He lived across the street from Steve on 32nd Street until he was about 16 when he and his family moved to Mattituck, on Eastern Long Island. This limited our contact with Danny until we got drivers' licenses and cars. A milestone that was very shortly followed by Danny enlisting in the Navy. He was still in the Navy when we had the party that included the picture taking session.

But in seventh grade Danny was a close friend. For some reason, we didn't separate Groups 1, 2 and 3 in seventh grade. Danny, a third grouper, and I, a first grouper were in a Social Studies class together. It was on a fine, sunny and warm late spring day, two periods before that day's dismissal and we were persevering through another episode of Sr. Appeline's circling and droning. Danny was in the second to last seat in the row nearest the windows trying not to be seen goofing around with another student.

Suddenly, the circling nun struck like a shark. Flailing and punching Danny from behind. She was boxing his ears and punching his shoulders. No tirade. No evil expression on her face. No anger. Not even an explanation. In fact, all that moved was her arms and shoulders.

At this very moment, Sr. Helen Marie walked to the door on a completely unrelated matter with a notebook and ruler in her hand. Seeing the beating in progress, she rushed to the back of the room and helped her sister Sister grab an arm and hustle Danny out to the hall.

Danny, at this time, was close to five feet ten inches tall. He was one of the biggest kids in class but the two nuns, four foot eleven and five two, were not put off by this size differential. At least that's how it sounded. The class was left alone and the door had been left open. We heard blows, slaps and groans coming from the hall. This may have lasted for 10 or 15 minutes, I'm not sure. But the bell did finally ring for us to change classes.

This was the first year that the students moved from class to class, rather than the teachers. You always stayed right. Trying to walk around an imaginary rectangle in the hall, one classroom on the schoolyard side and the other two on the Glenwood Rd side. Ours Social Studies class was in the room on the yard side.

We all got up to proceed to the next room on our rotation. Ready to stay to the right. Trying to behave like "Young Christian Teenagers".

What we saw was hardly a representation of that ideal.

Danny, towering over his attackers, was being held against the wall by Sr. Appeline's left hand on his right shoulder her right hand clenched in a fist. Sr. Helen Marie had a handful of shirt in her left hand and the ruler in her right. Not the infamous YADstick, but a wooden twelve inch ruler. And not like the flimsy things you get today, but a sturdy, thick solid oak wooden ruler. None of the three moved. Apparently, the bell had sounded the end of round one.

A round that Danny had lost, badly. He was a mess. One eye was already swollen. He was bleeding from out of his left ear and over his left eye. His tie knot was pulled open and the tie was stretched toward his left shoulder. His shirt was in complete disarray, the top three buttons open or missing.

Most of my classmates instinctively turned their heads toward their toes as soon as they got a look at Danny and walked quickly by. But Danny and I locked eyes. I'm sure my expression must have showed how horrified I felt, because his pained expression delivered a message to me loud and clear, "Help me. You're my friend, save me. Get me out of here." But I was paralyzed; with fear, anger, frustration and disgust.

Then Danny tried to lick his lips. The vividly terrible memory of the blood in his mouth, around the inside of his lips, staining his tongue and teeth will never leave me.

I was frozen with shock. First by the vision then by the conflict in my mind and soul.

The code says always cover your friends' back. Always be ready to help. You don't think of your own safety. You jump in if your friend needs it.

The code also says you must respect your elders. If they're older, you back down. Adults, especially clerical, know better. We never confronted adults and we saved a special position for those among us who had committed to a religious life. We trusted them to live up to the ideals that they were teaching us. Live up to the code and take care of those who were younger. I had become paralyzed by a conflict of principle that I had not been prepared for.

"Mr. Harwood, I believe you have a class to get to."

THE NUNS – PART 3

That was Sr. Marlita. Who had no idea of what was going on until she came out to the hall to monitor the class change. Once she saw what was happening, she hustled everyone to his or her next class so I don't know how the Danny incident ended that day.

But the aftermath? That went as follows.

The Principal and Pastor had an unpleasant meeting with Danny's parents. Danny was immediately transferred to Hudde JHS and never finished seventh grade with us and missed out on graduating the next year with the friends he had made in first grade.

Sisters Helen Marie and Appeline were sent to Coventry. Dominican HQ in Kentucky. Supposedly never to teach children again. I think that was Sr. Marlita's last term there also, but I don't think her leaving had anything to do with this.

As far as me, I learned then and there, before Sr. Marlita broke into my stupor, that the code was not pervasive. It didn't have all the answers. That some people didn't ascribe to it. Those of us who did, had to be diligent against people and events that defied it. It's a truism that we learn most when things go wrong. When there are problems. That's why this story is here. I learned more about people, the good in them and the bad, from these events in seventh grade. I learned more about how I should act from these events. But, I learned also that not doing something avoids

ramifications. That the squeaky wheel gets the grease. And that
sometimes that grease can be very unpleasant.

I learned there were cracks in the code. And the view could
get very ugly when you had the courage to look through one
of those cracks. But you had to look through if you were ever
going to fix it.

And I learned that we are all in it together. I vowed that I would
never allow any friend to endure what Danny had to that day. If
ever I see a vision of bloody teeth flash through my mind I know
it's time to act.

THE FIGHT

Even though there is a general reputation, unjustly earned, that Brooklynites get into a lot of fights, I don't think we fought any more than people from other places. We could, however, be counted on to face down any threat to a friend or any instance of injustice. And if that meant you had to fight, you fought. But, honestly, I avoided fights as much as I could. I actually never liked fighting. It always seemed to create more problems than it solved.

There was one exception, though.

About five years before we got married, and about six months after we started going out, my wife Mary, and her brother Danny, chipped in to buy a car. Sharing the use of a car wouldn't pose many problems for them because they could easily agree on the scheduling of who got the car which nights. They always had a good relationship. This included working together at the A & P Supermarket on Winthrop St and Nostrand Av, half a block from the house they grew up in before moving to Troy Av. and Farragut Rd.

They had gotten their jobs there because the manager of the A & P was a friend of their father's. When this story took place, Mary had just left her job at the supermarket to enter the Kings County Hospital Nursing School. Danny stayed on and even got two of his friends jobs there, one of who was known as JB.

JB and I didn't like each other much. We did eventually become pretty good friends a few years after this, but at this time we each had no use for the other.

I'm not sure what his problem with me was, but I found him to be a wise guy with an opinion of himself that was little higher than he deserved. I wouldn't be surprised if JB had the same kind of opinion of me.

My difficulty with JB boiled over after Mary had left the A&P and Danny became the store manager's preferred employee. Not a surprise because of Danny's ability, energy and dedication. It also probably involved the fact that Mary and Danny's father had died just before this and his good friend the manager tried to get Danny as many hours as he could to help out the family. A decent and correct thing to do.

But a couple of the other employees thought different.

JB and another guy named Pat became envious of the improved status Danny was enjoying and decided to get even. One night just before closing time at 10:00, they broke into the car, the one that both Mary and Danny shared, and removed the distributor cap, which they threw down a nearby sewer. Winthrop and Nostrand was not a good neighborhood at this time. Stranding Danny there, at the hour of the night they did it, was pretty a dangerous thing to do.

And it really pissed me off. It also pissed off a greater portion of the neighborhood.

I remember that Mary and I needed the car the next day and this vandalism also stranded us. But more importantly, JB and his accomplice, had punished Mary, and Danny, for a problem they had with their boss. Definitely, not the right thing.

Payback was due.

You may have heard a saying that has become popular in recent tough guy movies; 'Payback is a Bitch.' This is actually an excerpt from a truism everyone in Flatbush was brought up on. 'Do the Right Thing, because Payback is a Bitch'. The difference between the two statements is more than five words or any level of semantics. In Flatbush, the onus is on you. What you do, what you decide, how you coexist. There is no need to worry about payback if you do the right thing.

To those of us from Flatbush, 'Doing the Right Thing' was so important; that dispensing justified payback earned you a certain status. Poetic or creative payback was well respected in the neighborhood, possibly even made into legend if it was entertaining enough. Revenge taken at a petty complaint or enacted on an innocent was bogus. Not the right thing and an action to be reviled.

Not long after the weekend that JB and Pat committed their vandalism, a number of Mary's and Danny's friends, led by Lou, explained the 'Right Thing' concept to JB's accomplice, Pat. That 'Payback' session took the form of a short, one-sided episode of fisticuffs, administered solely by Lou. Now, Pat received his lesson, but nobody had seen JB.

Until I found him.

Mary and I were leaving Mahoney's one crisp, late autumn evening, when we saw JB in front of the travel agency, across E 42nd Street, talking to a friend nick-named Grandma. I felt that I was the right person, in the right spot, with the right message for JB. Mary told me she agreed, so I approached them. JB and Grandma knew what was coming, so Grandma, at least as close a friend of mine as JB's, took a step back.

I think a moment should be taken for me to offer some key statistics regarding the participants:

Grandma - about 6'1" and 235 lbs.

JB   - about 6'1" and 170 lbs.

Me   - about 5'8" and 165 lbs.

The travel agency had a storefront of about 20 – 25 feet wide, set back from the street by a 12 foot wide sidewalk. There was a door close to the store corner nearest E. 42nd St. and two large plate glass picture windows next to it. In front was parked a VW Carmen Ghia, the dumpy model smaller and lower than the Beetle.

I walked right up to JB, got into his face, and looked up and deep into his eyes and recited some stupid macho banter as his cost for not doin' the Right Thing. He responded with some equally stupid macho banter, followed by:

"So, what are you going to do about it!"

So I swung. A beautiful, arcing, as lethal as I'm capable, right-handed haymaker, pulled from the barn roof. The biggest right hand I had ever, or since, thrown.

And I missed.

But I recovered real fast. Before JB could respond, I grabbed his jacket at the lapels, and in my best hockey fight technique, lifted him back up off his heels and slammed him backwards into the boards, about 6 feet behind him.

But these boards shattered and became shards of glass flying all around us. We had crashed into the picture windows of the travel agency.

My mind started going at warp speed as soon as I realized that JB was headed through the window. I stopped his momentum, midair, and pulled him back out of the way of the falling glass, and then threw him across the sidewalk toward the street. Grandma and Mary, the only two witnesses seemed to be in shock. Neither had moved or said anything during the ten seconds or so since I had confronted JB. For a split second nobody moved or said anything. Then all four of us sprang into action at the same time. Mary turned and ran back to Mahoney's for help. JB, on his feet first, was coming back at me, I leapt up to respond, and Grandma tried to step in between us. He got there a split second too late.

Now it was JB's turn to throw his best punch. He didn't miss. He hit me square on the button. A good, solid, right hand, right on the chin.

And I didn't even blink.

Throughout my life I had been underestimated. Intellectually because of my efforts to hide from my intelligence. Physically, because I didn't cut such a swaggering figure. I am taller than I look. Heavier than I look. Faster than I look. Stronger than I look. But at that second, the instant after JB realized that I was smiling up at him after he had connected his best punch, right square on my chin, I knew that HE didn't underestimate me any longer. He had fear in his eyes. I had victory in mine. I knew right then, I had this fight won.

It was now time for JB's lesson in the 'Right Thing' and payback.

With my left hand I lifted JB onto his heels and flung him on his back on the front hood of the VW, right up against the windshield on the passenger side. As my first punch connected on his left cheekbone, I heard Grandma yell, "Okay, that's it! Break it up!"

Then my punching really started. I think I hit JB 12 – 15 times in all, every single punch hitting the same spot on his left cheekbone.

So far, I had put up a pretty impressive performance. This fight, I believe, gained for me a reputation that, thankfully, got me out of a number fights later on. But the part of the story that made this reputation had more to do with my struggle with Grandma than with JB.

Before my second punch had landed, Grandma tried to break us up by putting me in a headlock. The rest of the blows to JB's face came as Grandma was trying to drag me away. He only succeeded in sliding us along the round hood of the VW from the passenger to the driver side, JB pinned by me left hand, my right hand rising and falling like a piston.

My last punch never landed. JB had fallen off the hood and my left hand lost its grip, breaking my contact, easing my intensity and conquering my temper. Grandma and I stumbled out into the middle of Avenue D.

"That's it, Richie! No more!" Grandma screamed.

"Relax." I answered. "I'm fine." I was acting as if nothing had happened. My ripped shirt, heaving chest, and JB rolling on the ground trying to get his bearings showed that something had indeed happened. But my temper had instantly cooled as soon as my left hand lost its grip on JB's jacket. As soon as I lost contact with the culprit, the fight ended. Grandma was staring at me with disbelief. Not a second before I had been a red-eared pile driver robotically pummeling a larger man, while an even larger man was incapable of even slowing me down. But the second I was disconnected from my adversary, I had switched back to my relaxed real self.

At that same moment, my brother Tommy, Billy the bar manager and a few patrons were jogging over responding to Mary's alarm. Billy, whose opinion of JB was similar to mine, ran over to him and lifted him off the ground. "You're going to have to pay for that window, JB my boy." Billy said, as he was trying to signal for me to disappear with a nod.

"No way!" I said. "I threw HIM through that window. I broke it and I'm paying for it."

Everyone knew that I was going to have a lot of trouble with paying that claim since I was between jobs at this time – the time being right in the middle of Christmas shopping season. But they also knew that it was one of the purest statements of what I was defending by fighting JB. That JB's vandalizing of Mary's and Danny's car was so heinous, that if I allowed him to pay for that window I'd be guilty of the same injustice. I was having none of that.

Billy nodded. "You'll split it. JB, let's go into the bar. You too Richie."

As we walked back to the bar, Tommy asked me if I had got the better of the fight. Before I could answer, Grandma blurted out, "Holy spit, Tommy! The better of it! He picked him up, threw him through the window, then pulled him out before the glass fell! Took his best punch in the face without even flinching, and then threw him on the hood of the car and pounded the spit out of him as I was trying to pull him off! He kicked his ass!"

A big smile of pride grew on my brother's face. I kind of felt embarrassed at all the attention. Also, it bothered me a little that my own brother could underestimate me so much that he doubted the outcome. I don't know why, but I got very little satisfaction from that victory.

Whatever satisfaction I got came from the after-effects of the fight. Grandma, a noted storyteller whose fame came from how obviously he embellished certain facts, told as many people about this fight as he could. Somehow Grandma convinced a lot of those people that he wasn't exaggerating this time. An important factor because there was a lot of interest in how Mary and Danny's car was vandalized. It was widely known, and widely disapproved. It was generally accepted that justice would be meted out in due time. Pat got his justice from Lou, and now JB got his from me.

Probably because of that under estimating, a lot of people were surprised that I had won, but everyone was very surprised, and a little impressed, at HOW I won. In fact, I got the impression that by wigging out like I had, I gave people something to think about in the future. Whether this suspicion was true or not, or whether my fighting abilities were any good or not, I never did have to fight again after that. A very, very satisfying outcome.

But, the most satisfying part of this story came from me being a part of a community that rose up to defend one of our key principles.

The principle was clearly voiced as I shared a shot of whiskey with Lou that following weekend. A Mahoney's bartender named Jimmy paid for and delivered them to the duo of public defenders who had brought two villains to justice. As Lou and I raised the shots, Jimmy pronounced the following toast:

'Do the right thing, because payback is a bitch.'

Something everyone in hearing distance nodded their approval to.

EPILOGUE

Unbeknownst to me, Billy personally paid my half of the cost of that window. He got tired of making excuses as I was trying to give him money over the next few months and he finally told me he had paid it. I was forever grateful. This was just another in a long line of classy things that Billy did. In return, he could always count on me to cover the bar free of charge for him in an emergency, which usually involved an unexpected midnight call from a female friend. You do the right thing, not because payback is a bitch, but because it's the right thing.

P ART I I - C OURAGE

Having the courage to do the right thing might bring to mind
soldiers falling on a grenade. But that's a little too grand, and a
little too narrow, for what I'm talking about.

Looking someone in the eye and telling them a truth they don't
want to hear. Ignoring the taunts and ridicule of others when
making a decision that feels right for you. Self-confidence that
your dreams and beliefs DO matter. Looking in the mirror
and identifying the person their, warts and all, then seeing and
following the road that will allow your reflection to be the best
person possible. These all require courage and they're situations
all of us have been confronted with. Successfully applying this
courage leads each of us to our own path to excellence.

Having courage is our individual responsibility to a community
of excellence. Since our neighbors are supporting us in our life
we owe it to them to have the courage to identify our own
strengths and weaknesses, find our road to excellence and then
travel down that road as our personal contribution to the total
excellence within our community. This community excellence
is calculated as a sum total of all the individual 'excellences'

increased by the compound growth produced by the synergies of our interaction. "Your strengths covering my weaknesses so that I can follow my path and bring those successes back to everyone else". A whirlwind of interaction powering our community's voyage to excellence.

I'M WALKING OUTTA THIS PLACE

When I look down the roster of my family members, we all have had occasions requiring us to stand courageously in the face of life's tests. But one us, the oldest of Tom and Dorothy's nine children, was faced with an event that pales all others in comparison. That would be my brother Tommy. Generally accepted as one of the really good guys from Flatbush and generally considered our best football player. In 1975 TH was a good-looking guy with a lot going for him.

Especially courage.

That summer, when Tommy was about 23 years old, he took a trip to visit one of his best friends who had moved to Maryland. That friend, Tiger, had gone to school in West Virginia and stayed down there with his soon-to-be bride. With two other friends, TH piled into his mint 1955 Olds 88 for the 6 or 7 hour ride to join Tiger and company for an Independence Day party and barbecue in the remoter hills of Maryland.

The ride down turned out fine but the party did not.

It was taking place at a small cabin on a narrow dirt road right by a small lake with still, cloudy water that reflected the image of the tree-clad hills surrounding the home that was to house the celebrants. Beautiful scenery, but a bit off the beaten path. Not a bad site for a boisterous Fourth of July barbeque.

After the long sweaty ride, there was no air conditioning in the 88, Tommy's first thought was to go for a quick swim. After changing into a swimsuit, he came out of the cabin and starting running toward the lake, currently populated by about 8 people in chest deep water. TH ran quickly out the door, quickly across the porch, and quickly down the bank to dive in.

He made one very crucial mistake - the other bathers were sitting, not standing, as he had thought. He dove while running at full speed just as we do to enter the Atlantic Ocean surf at Riis Park back in New York. Leaping as far out and with as much power as his speed and athletic ability could generate. Head first. Head first into a submerged rock that halved the depth of the already shallow water. His neck shot with electric pain, his body went completely numb, he started floating, face down in the water, unable to move, holding his breath, hoping someone would realize he was not fooling around and come save him. Becoming terrified that no one would.

To his great fortune, someone did. She was a nurse. Sitting in the water with her was a large, powerful man, who, closely following the nurse's instructions, gently rolled Tommy over so he could breath, but cradled TH in his arms without jostling him.

This was the first in a series of miraculous coincidences that might make this story a little difficult to believe, and, if believed, suggests evidence that we do indeed have divine intervention in our lives.

Once the nurse in the water determined that my brother couldn't move, she gave her rescue assistant instructions about how to hold but not move the victim, and ran full speed to the cabin to get a friend, another nurse, who she felt knew more about taking care of people with these kind of injuries. They quickly decided that they needed to get TH to an emergency room real fast. To do that they had to immobilize his head and secure him in the back of a van that was to stand in as an ambulance and then clear the one lane dirt road of parked cars so it could get out quick and clean. They succeeded in immobilizing Tommy's head by strapping him to a board. He was then safely installed in the van, which began the mad dash to the small, nearby, community hospital. The van's exit being helped by the cars being rushed to the main road with their emergency blinkers on to block any oncoming traffic giving the van a clean exit from the dirt road. It made it to the hospital in record time.

After a second or two of confusion, the Emergency Room staff responded very quickly to the bikini clad woman who ran in and started reciting technical jargon just ahead of four men struggling to gently carry a young man who was strapped to a piece of wood. The ER doctor, after a few seconds of diagnosis, ran to the phone to recall the helicopter that had taken off just moments before, to come back and pick-up TH. He was speedily transferred onto the helicopter for the return journey to its home base, The University of Maryland, at Baltimore, Medical Center.

Within minutes of his injury, Tommy was flying to the home of one of only two existing Shock/Trauma units in the country at this time. The other being in Los Angeles, Ca.

The Shock/Trauma unit was a hi-tech, research/treatment center that specialized in severe accident and athletic injuries, like a broken neck.

Which was what Tommy had.

This athletic, good-looking, popular guy, who was scheduled to enter the Fire Department of New York Academy, his dream job, not a few weeks later, was now staring at being paralyzed for the rest of his life. Confronted with having all his hopes and dreams destroyed forever. He had every right to start complaining and bemoaning the cruel fate that sentenced him to this unfair turn of events. He easily might have become depressed and start feeling totally defeated.

What was his response?

"I'm walking out of this place!" he said.

He said it loud and he said it often. He said it to anyone who was near. He said it every chance he got. He never stopped saying it. The doctors and nurses always smiled and nodded and made him feel like they believed this as much as he did. Even though they didn't. But they did know that if TH believed it, then it might be possible. So they kept encouraging this thought even as they adjusted the 120lbs of traction screwed into his skull to keep his vertebrae separated. The aim of the traction was to minimize the damage to his spinal cord as it swelled from the injury and rubbed against the vertebrae. They smiled and playfully tickled his toes or pushed up against his foot to test his response. They exchanged jokes with Tommy when they came back every three hours to spin him from face down to face up, or vice versa, on the Striker bed which is specially designed to improve his circulation and prevent bed sores.

His surgeon was a great guy who did not let his professional renown distract him from recognizing that his patients were people with feelings and fears and not just a series of symptoms. He showed this by allowing Tommy an occasional bottle of Heineken with his dinner.

As great a guy as this doctor was, it came as no surprise to us that Tommy's closest relationships were with the nurses. We expected this partly because of his personality, partly because of a nurse's natural dedication to her patients recovery, and partly because these particular professionals relied on their hearts as well as their training, education and expertise to deal with patients who had to come to grips with life changing trauma. They took great pains to always comfort, encourage, and support TH as he went through the recovery period, even though most felt certain that, at best, he would spend the rest of his life in a wheelchair.

But the environment, the treatments, and the courage of my brother to stay positive were powerful forces. After a few hours of surgery and 24 days of treatment, and on my nineteenth birthday, TH had my father wheel him down to the Shock/ Trauma Center from his Post/OP recovery room on the 17th floor to say goodbye to all the wonderful people who had helped him overcome this horrible injury. Incredibly, he was going home the next morning.

But not before giving them a goodbye gift.

As they were leaving, Tommy had my father stop the wheelchair about ten feet before the doors leading out of the Center back to the elevators, he then got up from his wheelchair and without looking back, gingerly paced off the steps needed to walk through those doors, delaying his exit for just a second to offer a wave over his shoulder. I had tears in my eyes when one of the nurses told me about this a few months later. I had tears in my eyes when I wrote the first draft of this story in pencil. I have tears in my eyes as I type this.

But, not nearly half as many tears as those nurses and doctors had when they watched him 'Walk Out Of That Place.'

S L E E P O V E R

Please refer back to the cover photo to the man standing second from the left. This is Phil. What an expression! You would be right to assume that this man likes to be in charge and lead us on some merry adventures. Phil was always someone who looked for the boundaries, who liked to test authority and question the rules. But once he determined that that authority or rule was proper he was equally emphatic about complying with and defending its righteousness.

What's less obvious in that expression is the expansive artistic talent that Phil possesses. He has had his artwork published on movie posters, billboards, magazine illustrations and most notably, golf instruction drawings. It can take a bit of an adjustment to accept Phil's talents if your knowledge of him comes from the athletic field or our partying. But those of us who know him best are very comfortable with both 'Phil's' because he has been very true to each of his seemingly conflicting personalities for his entire life. He came to realize early in life what his talents and weaknesses were and he has had the courage to follow a path to success that they lent themselves to. Of our group of friends, Phil, far and away more than any other, epitomizes my definition of courage and could be counted on to be true to himself and to seek out ways to test that self.

Phil has a massive 'bold' streak. He liked to confront all life had to offer and was never one to sit comfortably aside and watch events play themselves out. He seemed to always manage to be in the forefront of the things we did, planned or otherwise. He had the courage to do and the courage to accept responsibility for what he did.

Except once.

As is often said, exceptions prove the rule. You will read a number of examples of Phil leading the way in confronting the world. But here is one time his discretion got the better of his valor.

Phil's brother Tommy threw a party one beautiful summer Saturday night. The night was beautiful not only because of the weather but also because their parents would be staying with relatives on Long Island.

Tommy was one of the most popular guys in our neighborhood, and in a lot of other neighborhoods, too. He had a smile that could light up a Lenten prayer meeting at a Jesuit Monastery and the dance steps to get even a monk up and boogying. Plus he had a reputation as one of the best people to party with in Brooklyn. They came from all corners of Brooklyn for this one.

Add to that crowd, us, and some of our friends, and this party quickly got good. Good and crowded. The crowd started spreading to the back porch, down into the backyard, to the front stoop, the driveway and even upstairs to the hallway. The mob scene went everywhere but to Phil's bedroom/studio in the basement. It got a little tight so to get a little air, we wound up down there. It was a good place because this site allowed us to foray through the three doors that led, respectively, to the backyard, the front stoop, and upstairs to the kitchen where the beer was stored. We could stay connected with the party and yet find sanctuary when the elbow-to-elbow crowding got too tense.

About 1:00 am Phil came down from the kitchen and privately asked me what I instantly considered a strange question, "Can I sleep at your house tonight?" This was strange because we never did this in our lives. Not just Phil and I, but nobody. The distance from one house to the other was always so close; we could walk just about anywhere. So, sleepovers weren't popular. To get from Phil's house to mine you had to walk up East 37th St about 100 yards, cross Farragut Road, and then cross East 37 Street and walk about another 50 yards.

"Sure, no problem" I replied. Easy answer because my parents had moved to Pennsylvania and left the yet to be sold house with my two older brothers and I.

"Good. Let's go." He said.

"Now?"

"Yeah, it's too crowded here." He explained.

We went upstairs through the kitchen, got four beers each, then muscled our way through the shoulder to shoulder crowd, over the beer soaked dining room carpet, over the beer soaked living room carpet, past the 8 people in the 3ft by 4ft vestibule, and the twenty or so people on the porch and stoop, and then, to my surprise, directly across 37th Street. We turned and started the 150 yard walk on my side of 37th St across Farragut Road to my house. Phil being especially conscious of any cars that turned down the street. This is the only time in my recollection that that walk wasn't made on his side of 37th Street until we crossed Farragut Rd. I was a little confused. But I didn't say anything.

Once we were safely tucked in my living room he told me what was up.

It seems Phil heard that his mother had called at about 11:30 to check on things and was told by an unfamiliar voice that she, the voice, didn't know anyone by the name of Tommy, and hung up. A repeat call confirmed the worst when it was rudely and profanely disconnected by the same voice.

Judging that the ride from Long Island would take about 1and a half hours, Phil needed to escape quickly and quietly. This explained why we didn't tell Chris, Steve or Joe R, or Tommy, or anyone else where we were going. Plus, it explained why we crossed the street in front of his house instead of nearer to the corner as usual.

All for confronting what life had to offer, but Phil was not so bold as to confront his mother and father once they stepped onto those rugs.

But Phil couldn't escape his inborn penchant for doing the right thing. His contribution to that party required him to stand next to his brother Tommy and take responsibility for their parents' anger. The next morning we went back to help with the clean up and to share the blame that was up till then shouldered by Tommy alone.

FRIENDSHIP

By the time I reached the sixth grade my 'place' with my classmates was pretty well determined. I was one of the smartest in my class, one of the top athletes, and one of the top 2 targets of jokes and rank outs. I got ranked on more than anyone else, except one girl who traveled in a different circle. Looking back, the reasons for this had a lot more to do with me and how I acted than my friends and how they did.

The first reason was that I took extra delight in being right. Being pretty smart and having the big mouth I had, there were frequent incidents where I emphatically impressed on my friends I was right, so they were wrong. On almost any subject. This earned me the nickname of the 'Walking Encyclopedia'. So my friends were very happy to give me an extra hard time on the rare occasion when I was wrong. They regularly took shots at me, I believe, to reaffirm their own self-respect, of course, at the expense of mine. They also showed this by giving me more nicknames then anybody else, almost all of them being derogatory. Besides the 'Walking Encyclopedia', there was 'Roach', derived from my first name and my lack of size,

'Hardware, hardhead, hard-just-about-anything, because of my last name.

Second, I mainly hung out with the guys who weren't by and large in the 'smarter' part of the class. My childhood friends were the other guys that played football, baseball and basketball. The jocks. Only one or two of who were with me in Group 'I'. These few didn't merit the same negative attention as me because they were normal sized, average athletes and definitely not as much of a big mouth. Besides, I was kind of used to being the brunt of jokes, so I added to my attractiveness as an easy target by being an accepting victim.

Accepting victim or not, deep down, I hurt from all the demeaning attention, as well as you might expect.

I can't express to you how important it was to me to do things that they would appreciate. Do whatever I could to try and stop the name-calling. However, I could never connect with the reality of my situation. As intense was my need for acceptance, my efforts always excluded calming my mouth down, but eventually included doing less than my best at my schoolwork. I was able to maintain a 93 average over my eight years in St. Vincent Ferrer even though I had stopped reading, studying and doing any homework somewhere about third or fourth grade. All I accomplished with this effort to remake myself into someone more acceptable to them was to take away from my own sense of accomplishment and thereby increase my exposure to my friends' insults. I suppressed so many things that were important to me to try and eliminate those personal traits that were the inspiration for my friends' rank outs but never getting it right. I was stuck in a whirlpool of pain and unable to see that the relief resided in just being more naturally myself.

But, then the new guy came.

His name was Ray. Ray had transferred in from St. Jerome's, one parish over. He looked lonely as he sat quietly in a seat next to me; probably feeling a little bit lost in his new school. I was the first person to start talking to him in class. It was only a matter of days before we started hanging out together after school.

I was finally having a good time when I went out after school. Every day, something about Ray made me more excited about spending more time with him. We had a lot in common. He felt more comfortable with the athletic guys, just as I did. Just like me, Ray didn't need to do his homework to get 90's (and just like me he didn't do his homework).

But our differences were even more compelling. Ray had a weird sense of humor and unusual interests. Unlike just about anybody else, he was able to surprise me, to make me laugh with the unexpected. He introduced me to science fiction and to different music, new things to me, things that I couldn't act like an 'Encyclopedia' about. But most important, Ray didn't make fun of me. So, we became friends.

In just a few weeks Ray decided to introduce me to some of his old friends at St. Jerome's. I first met them at their park, Foster Park, when we went there to play football. This park was behind a schoolyard for a public school on Nostrand Avenue between Foster Avenue and Farragut Road. But the park didn't quite make it all the way to Farragut Road so it had an unusual approach down the 31st/32nd horseshoe-shaped street. Not being able to see it from Farragut Road, I had forgotten this park was there. A mere five short blocks away from home and between my old apartment and the school I spent my two weeks of Kindergarten.

Most of the guys I met through Ray became pretty good friends of mine about 7 years later, but then, they weren't overly thrilled to have Ray bring some big mouth, encyclopedic, athletic shrimp from St. Vinnie's who could outplay most of them at football. It seemed their unhappiness about me made Ray feel a lot better.

Outcasts Unite!

The St. Jerome's crowd (I won't use the term 'gang' because that word has a specific meaning that did not apply to them or us) did find a good way to get even; they challenged the St. Vinnies crowd to a football game, at their park, using their rules. The site and rules were important because this gave them a decided advantage. We always played our football games at 'J' Park, a dirt field. Foster Park was asphalt. This fact created different football games. Different plays requiring different talents. Their game put more emphasis on throwers and receivers than blockers and runners. We were real good at blocking, at running, at tackling, and at defending a run based offense, but not too many of us could play end. I could catch passes, but I was a better halfback then wideout because I had a great move for tackle football. All I had to do was get the defender chasing me in one direction and then suddenly cut back into his trailing hip. Being lower to the ground and initiating the contact I had the greater power and would usually run through the tackle. Their game was two-hand touch. My power move wouldn't work because the defender only had to touch me with two hands to 'tackle' me. Obviously, new techniques would be needed.

Of the other guys on my team, there was one very good athlete, better than everyone else there. That was John. He was the biggest guy on our team, he could throw well, run well, block well, etc. John would later become an All-city High School football player for Midwood H.S. He was our best end and our best quarterback. But even he hadn't figured out how to be both on the same play.

We played the game early on a Saturday morning. They actually had a real referee there. Well, maybe not real, but he was an adult and he called penalties and enforced the rules. But, it wasn't long before we were losing. Badly. Other than John and I, the guys on our team weren't able to contribute too much, so the game turned into their eight men against John and I. Since our teammates had no role in the game, they started whining, complaining, and ultimately, leaving. I was convinced they blamed me for this fiasco and left out of disgust. But I later found out the real reason was that they discovered that after the game the St. Jerome's guys wanted to fight.

Fighting was not as popular at St.Vinnie's as it was at St. Jerome's. My classmates who were not in the game didn't want to fight, so they starting leaving two at a time to avoid any problems. Just after I noticed this exodus, I twisted my ankle. Now things got worse. If I left the game, it would be 8 on 7 (they also had 2 reserves). I couldn't continue with the pain but John and the others wanted to keep playing. So, to try and do both, I would play certain plays and then stand on the sidelines for few plays, and then rejoin the game. Repeating this iteration until, finally, I gave in to the pain and just left.

To leave I had to walk to the gate at the foot of 31st Street. We were playing on a field on the far end of the park and closer to 32nd St.. It took me a while to limp the 200 yards or so to the gate. When I exited and turned to continue toward 32nd St I could see back through the fence. It appeared that after I had left the game had ended, but then the fight had begun. Well, sort of. The fight was half-hearted, at best. I saw the 11 or so of the St. Jerome's guys following John and his 6 teammates as they traced the same path I had just used. There were small pushes and shoves now and then, but no takers. My friends just kept walking steadily toward the gate.

Now I had a new dilemma. Seeing the impending fight, I argued with myself on whether to go back or not.

The argument against returning; why would they need a small guy like me? With my ankle the way it is? Besides, these were the guys who tortured me day in and day out. They don't need me - and even if I did help, they wouldn't care. It wouldn't change anything. Maybe, them getting in a fight right in front of me would feel good to the guy they picked on the most.

But two thoughts completely wiped out any argument about not going back.

First, I had arranged the game. I had put both sides together. I really hated fights but I had the responsibility to be there to the end.

Second, these guys were my friends. Since first grade, some even before that. No matter how bad their ranking, you never lose a friend's back. Not in Flatbush. Not the way we were brought up.

So, I did the right thing and went back.

As I got closer to the undulating mass of eleven-year-olds, it became apparent why the fight was so half-hearted. Only two or three of the guys on the other team really wanted to fight. The others seemed to gain a level of respect for the guys who stuck the game out until the end and didn't run. Besides that, none of them really wanted any part of John, who was a pretty intimidating kid. He was making sure that he stayed between his friends and the belligerents. Because John was the closest to them he was taking the brunt of the insults. But he never got mad. He never answered any of the insults. Since neither of the two loudmouths would move past John and the others from St. Jerome's didn't want the fight, we were able to exit the park and head home without any incident.

They stopped following us at the gate. We passed out, turned left and started to head home.

John only said one thing as we walked back. "Leave him alone."

The rest of my teammates had been yelling and cursing at me, blaming me for all the problems. So I became content to occupy the last file in our small troop of vanquished footballers. They took turns to turn their heads and blast me as I limped along behind. But John stopped that. I quickly lost track of whether anything else was said because I started to straggle. My ankle was throbbing. Even if they still had things to tell me, I didn't want to say or hear anything. Being invisible right now seemed like a very good idea. My spirits were pretty low. My idea of a great football game had become an utter mess. My classmates now had something else to be mad at me about. I expected to get a new level of torture at school that Monday.

After I reached the first corner, I looked up to see that they had gotten a full block ahead of me. It was going to be a long, lonely, painful walk home. It would have been nice to have at least one person to walk with me. They wouldn't have to say anything, just be there.

Wait a minute. Where's Ray? Just then I remembered. Ray had acted pretty strange that day. He had started the game on our team. When we started losing, he switched to their team. But he wasn't on either team at the end. He had left. As a matter of fact, he was one of the first to leave when the talk of a fight first started.

Now I knew why Ray was an outcast. He was a coward. He wasn't my friend, he wasn't their friend, he wasn't anyone's friend. He was the one lost, pained, and alone. He didn't understand about covering a friend's back. That what you do when things get rough. That's what shows your friendship. How well you do when you're needed.

But I did have a friend. Actually, I had a lot of them. They gave me a rough time. Made fun of me. Made up names about me. But, they stuck by me in spite of all the noise. And, today when I had a choice, I stuck by them. Then John stuck by me by getting them to leave me alone. They agreed, in fact, they agreed so much so that I didn't hear one word on Monday from those friends who were there to the end.

I really felt guilty about those negative thoughts I had about my friends as I considered leaving that park. They had always given me a hard time and now that I thought I had found someone who I could be loyal with I doubted their friendship. I thought I had found one guy who understood what it was like to be the person everyone laughed at. I thought I had found a new friend.

But Ray didn't understand what a friend is. Being there when things are fun is easy. Being there when things are rough is a big part of friendship. The big difference between Ray and I was he never would have gone back. He never felt responsible for the game, the fight or his friends. He didn't have the courage to do the right thing when the right thing is most needed.

But, John did understand when he prevented his friends from fighting back after the game. So did the guys on the St. Jerome's team. Especially those that didn't want to fight. They stuck together making sure they covered each other's backs. And they still had the courage to do the right thing by us. The St. Vinnie's kids that stayed to the end had earned their respect. We had earned the right to leave in peace. We often think of courage as the ability to be brave and fight with all our might when in combat. Sometimes it takes courage not to fight. When it is the right thing.

SCARED STRAIGHT

Like everywhere else in America during the 70's, there were drugs in Flatbush. Luckily, though, in our corner of the world, there were very few people who got into the heavy stuff, like heroin. We did have some who would take pills and some even had problems with cocaine. But, just about everybody in this era tried marijuana at least once.

Marijuana was not the end unto itself. Using that, or beer, or wine, etc was not the attraction. They were used to help with the good times. Adding to the community feeling of hanging out. Most were like me, tried it and dismissed it for a combination of moral and practical reasons. This is a story about someone who dismissed it for another reason.

One thing to remember, its not just the cool people I'm talking about here, the nerds tried pot too. Nerds, dorks, whatever title you give them, are like all of us. They have the same needs and the same wants as everybody else, just different priorities. This doesn't make them bad, only different. We had nerds in Brooklyn, in fact some of them became pretty good friends of mine. This is a story about three nerds and their adventure with marijuana (which for brevity's sake, will now be referred to as pot; easier to type.)

Two of our heroes smoked pot fairly frequently but bachelor #3 DID NOT. As a matter of fact, he had a real problem that his two best friends DID. They argued about it a lot.

"Its illegal, it's a sin, its wrong!" Nerd #3 would say.

"Just try it. You'll see. Then you'll know. How can you condemn something you don't know anything about?" Countered N1 and N2.

This went on for months, possibly years. Until, finally, the 'Try It' chorus in tandem started to wear N3 down. He relented and agreed to at least try it. As a matter of fact, they were to do it that very weekend. Maybe to N3 sinning is more serious on a weekday.

Actually, these were not card-carrying, full-fledged pocket protector nerds. They were pretty typical guys who just had a few dork tendencies. All were very smart and all were pretty good athletes. But they didn't have fun the ways that were most common in Flatbush liking hanging out at a bar. Usually they went to someone's house to listen to music or maybe even go to a movie. Their contact with the rest of the world almost always took place at a single particular diner. So, I guess we can cut N3 some slack about some of his naïve ideas about pot, especially the sin part.

N1 and N2 decided that since N3 was their best friend, they were expected to help make his maiden marijuana voyage memorable. To do this they needed to plan the details carefully.

First, they thought about where.

N1's house? N2's house?

Wouldn't work due to some parent issues that couldn't be overcome on such short notice.

Just walking around?

No, that would be too much work. They needed to be able to relax.

N1's car?

After various other options were proposed and rejected, they settled on N1's car. That way they could also have the right music.

What music? Easy. 'Tommy' by the Who.

But since they couldn't get a record player in the car they'd have to rely on a tape player. The technology of the day seriously limited a car's ability to support hi-fi music. Almost all cars only had an AM radio back then. If you had FM radio that meant that you went high hog on the car's options. And, if you wanted to get really funky, you got yourself an 8-track cassette player. Therefore, this dorkish cabal had to settle on a little reel-to-reel recorder that had to tape 'Tommy' acoustically; by putting a mike in front of the speakers, instead of electronically. This was all about two steps up from Fred and Barney, but it would have to be good enough.

So now they were all set, they had the right setting, N1's car. The right music, 'Tommy'. They even bought some extra, extra virgin, A-one, hi-grade utmost quality pot. The Good Stuff.

Everything was going along perfectly.

Well, almost.

These very intelligent, extensively prepared, nerdly heroes, dedicated to the cultural advancement of their best friend, decided to park the now designated 'Partymobile' at the park. Farragut Park. (Really Paerdagett Park, but by this time we all called it Farragut Park after the street). Right on the corner of 40th Street. Three blocks from home and a spot that was constantly patrolled by police who usually rode around on scooters.

The big mistake they made was to take themselves out of their natural element without a guide. Hanging out at the park was something foreign to these three. Even though each had at least one brother who used Farragut Park as their headquarters, they themselves usually went to someone's house for their entertainment. Therefore, they were ill-prepared to judge if any warning signs were flashing when they approached their chosen spot. The most obvious omen that they missed was that the park was deserted. "It was too quiet."

Usually on a weekend night you could count on a few dozen people sitting by the softball backstop right on the corner they were parked at. Also, even more reliable were the few dozen more who hung out at the basketball courts halfway up 40th St., which they had to pass on the way to their spot. This night, the only things stirring at any point in the park were the crickets.

So, right in the middle of smoking their first joint, N3 having received the pot for his second hit, the Fourth of July erupted.

Lights flashing!!! Cars careening!!! "Out of the Car" and "Hands where I can see 'um" being screamed!!! Blocked by a police car in front!!! Blocked by a police car in back!!! Police to the left of them!!! Police to the right of them!!! Police all around them!!!

It seems for the police, this was a special night too. They weren't on patrol, they were on stakeout. Stakeout for two nerds who were introducing their best friend to the many wonders of pot, while listening to the right music, in the right vehicle, parked in the wrong location?

Not hardly.

They were staked out for a pair of thieves who were breaking into the houses that bordered the park along Farragut Rd and down 40th St. All the park regulars knew about the stakeout because of a guy called Bibba. His mother worked at the police precinct and would warn him to stay out of the park on the nights of heightened police activity there. He would then pass the word.

It didn't take the police very long to realize that they did not have the burglars they were looking for. It was three, untroublesome neighborhood nerds with three joints who just happened to pick the wrong spot to get high. Actually, one of the cops involved later told us that they were trying very hard not to laugh when they heard the details of this maiden attempt at pot smoking for N3. I think the cops decided that in good conscience they shouldn't take this very seriously.

So, ID's were checked but no records were made. The joints were confiscated but the three people were released after being issued stern warnings.

As if they needed it.

N3 was still as petrified as anyone could get. His life flashed before his very eyes. All his aspirations, all his possibilities would be gone, because he weakened. He allowed his friends to seduce him into committing a sin he had sworn he would never do. And he would never do it. Never again! He had committed himself to a path to success and this close brush with catastrophe only reaffirmed his determination to courageously follow that path no matter what anyone else thought.

I'M COOL

At various points in this book I'm going to describe certain incidents where we had to deal with policeman, or better said, the police had to deal with us. The stunts, rather than crimes, we committed were totally innocent - and only done in the spirit of having some harmless fun. We acted totally without malice.

The part of all these stories that I feel best about is that they allow me to highlight the excellent behavior of the police. By and large, they grew up in the neighborhood too. And for the most part, they also learned, taught and lived by the code. They were really very good at being able to differentiate between neighborhood kids who might have gone a little too far with some harmless stunt and the really troubled kids who needed official attention. I'm happy to say that none of my friends comes to mind as having needed official attention.

Chronologically, this is the first of the incidents where the police had to pay us some attention and showed why they are called New York's Finest. A curious coincidence of these incidents is that we came away from each of these encounters with a classic line from Phil. I guess it helped Phil's comic creativity if the energy of a police confrontation was included to activate his unique genius.

This first police confrontation occurred just after Halloween, 1973. That evening's most recurring topic of discussion was Steve's very strange activities that previous holiday. Though these antics might have seemed strange for anyone else, we were quickly getting used to very strange things following Steve. Couple this with the typical eeriness of Halloween night and it's no wonder Steve's actions would dominate our conversations. Unfortunately, I can't remember the details of Steve's antics.

Instead of sitting at our usual spot in Farragut Park, we were walking from there to Michaels Bar with the remnants of our 8 packs of Bud. We each had maybe a beer or two left. We left the comfort of the park because Bibba again had warned us that the police were going to do another sweep that night. Bibba's mother's warning had again successfully completed its circuit of our emergency communications network.

The route to Michael's took us up 40th Street to Glenwood Rd., then a right on Glenwood toward Michael's, which was on Ave H between 34th and 35th, one more long block up and 5 short blocks over. Since I wasn't going to Michaels, my companions decided to stop at the parish library yard on the corner of 38th and Glenwood to finish the beers without deserting me. The library, located across Glenwood Rd from the church, was actually an old house on two plots that had a large yard with plenty of bushes and trees. The deceased woman who last lived here left it to the church. The pastor converted it into a library when the original one was razed to make room for building the new school.

Actually, it was really odd that we would stop here. We never did it before and never since. It was not a usual hangout. It just seemed a conveniently cozy place to spend the time needed to finish two nips before passing on to where each of us was going to go: me, the short trip of a block down to 37th Street for home and the rest of them the last four blocks to Michaels.

Once in the yard, we split up into two groups. Dougie, a different Richie, Jerry and Joe R under an exterior stairway from the second floor on the 38th Street side of the house. Phil, Chris, Steve and I in the back around a small mound at the center of the garden behind the house. The stair guys could place their bottles on the steps for easy access and we could sit on the mound for a little bit of comfort.

It was pretty warm for an early November night so sitting around outside wasn't going to be a problem unless we forgot ourselves and got too loud.

We were there maybe a half hour when I asked Jerry and found out that it was now 11:15 pm. My curfew was actually 11:00, but I had manipulated it to about 11:20 by stretching my arrival time over a period of months. But I never let myself go overboard with this stretching activity.

"You've got to learn how to train your father." Said Phil extolling the virtues of his philosophy on pushing boundaries to see how far they could be stretched.

He was trying to convince me to stay later and go with them to Michael's. Say, until 12:00. Get into a little more trouble tonight, but then come home next weekend at 11:30 and then steadily increase the curfew over the subsequent weekends. I wasn't really interested in testing my father on that level. Besides, I had too much respect for him to try and finagle things in this fashion. Twenty minutes was the most I was ready to push things at this time.

I tried to explain this to Phil being very careful to keep my volume under control. He wasn't very impressed but, because I didn't want to argue myself into being late, I put aside any further discussion and bid them all a fond adieu.

Having already said goodbye to the guys under the stairs, they had the watch, I turned my back on Phil's argument, hopped the fence to the next yard, ran down the driveway, across the neighbor's lawn and hurried all the way home. The run probably taking me about two minutes to complete. Phil had wasted about three of my five minute cushion so I had to hustle to get home 'in time', if not 'on time'. My father did have a comment about my arrival time but he accepted my apology and I went to bed. Another night of my usual fitful tossing and turning between hour-long stints of sleep. My mind, as usual, was a whirlwind of images and philosophical questions keeping me awake half the night.

Boy did I miss the real excitement.

According to a number of my remaining 7 friends, at the same instant that I scaled the fence, the front gate opened and two plains clothes policemen entered the yard, with their guns drawn. Drawing their guns was a very rare occurrence around Flatbush. They must have been concerned about being outnumbered 8 to 2.

"Alright, you guys, don't move, come out where we can see you. Line up against the wall." They barked orders to the 'Understairs guys'.

Overhearing the commands, the guys in the back, Steve, Chris, Phil and now Joe R, went into maneuvers.

They each fled to a hiding spot. Steve, Joe R and Chris all hopped the fence as I did and just lay down in the tall weeds. Phil also started for the line of bushes paralleling the fence but stopped short of climbing over. Phil didn't like this spot, so he scanned the garden and decided he would be better off on the other side of the yard by a big bush near the garage. He felt he could make the dash unnoticed because the route was behind a large bushy tree in the middle of the yard.

He was wrong.

"FREEZE!!" called out the authoritative police voice. Some witnesses actually believe he added "Or I'll shoot!"

Phil stopped dead in his tracks. A pretty good feat considering how fast Phil could run. His hands went just as instantaneously to the back of his head, his bag of empty nips continuing on its forward path crashing and spilling open a good five yards in front of him.

"I'm cool." He shouted. (The classic line).

Alright, I have to admit, I wasn't overly impressed with the 'classicness' of this line. Phil's has had a lot that were much better. Whether you or I think so isn't very important, either. What is important was that Chris and Steve thought so. They both started laughing as soon as they heard it, giving away their positions. Actually, the cop only heard Steve.

"Okay, you too." The cop said to Steve.

"Aw, damn." Said Steve, extremely disappointed that his hiding spot wasn't as good as he at first thought. "How'd you know I was there?" But as he said this, he stepped on Joe R who was lying, as yet unnoticed, just in front of Steve. "Oh, sorry Joe." Came Steve's unconscious reaction.

This line was Chris' undoing.

He couldn't control himself after Phil's classic and Steve's typically unconscious lines. He stood up on his own and came out with his hands showing and his head shaking.

Now I love Chris like a brother, but for the life of me I can't to this day understand why he did this. Joe R or Phil either. I have never, ever even tried to understand the things Steve does.

Being a Monday morning quarterback, I reminded them that Chris' backyard was about 15 to 20 feet away from the hiding place they were in. If they wanted to escape, all they had to do was hop the same fence I did, go behind the garage and hop the fence behind Chris' garage and then quickly duck down his basement.

They defended themselves by saying that since they weren't doing anything wrong they weren't prepared to work out an escape route. I really should cut them more slack on this because I doubt I would have done any differently. Plus, they didn't think they could have made it safely from a cop with a gun.

Still, I would have liked for them to have escaped. But that would have ruined the rest of this story. So I guess it's just as well that Chris, Steve, Phil and Joe R handled this just as they had.

The two cops marched all seven 'prisoners' out the gate in front and piled them into the back seat of the police car. A seat designed to seat 3, maybe 4 comfortably. The college frat-like stunt was accomplished by seating six shoulder to shoulder and Joe R lying across their laps.

They had to give their names and addresses. The police taking special notice that all seven lived within seven blocks of the library, six of them within two blocks. Plus, all of the addresses were within the parish boundaries. They were having doubts they had caught the heinous criminals they were staked out for.

"What were you doing?"

"Just finishing up a couple of beers before going home."

They asked about break-ins to the library and were convincingly reassured by all seven that books were not highly valued by any of them at this points in their lives. Especially not religious books.

The cops moved away from the car to discuss their dilemma in private. They were looking for people who were breaking in to the library and these seven were definitely not the culprits. But they were trespassing, even if they were not creating a disturbance or vandalizing anything. The cops didn't want the pastor to complain to their boss about a lack of progress in their investigation. Still, they had trespassers in custody, but, come on, one of them practically lived right next door.

Their discussion was rudely interrupted.

While they were trying to figure out the best way to handle this, the prisoners started to riot. Well, not exactly riot, but they were screaming and opening windows and stretching their heads coughing and gagging for clean air.

Joe R had farted.

In the middle of this disturbance, six voices rose up in chorus:

"CHRIS, SHUT THE FLICK UP!!!!"

What was going on inside the 'paddy wagon' that created the seeming insurrection was Chris sitting against the far door, slowly shaking his head as it was clutched in his hands and constantly repeating, "I'm dead. I'm friggan' dead." Over and over, again and again. Each of his compatriots had taken a turn to try to reassuringly comfort him that everything would be okay. "We didn't do anything wrong. Calm down. We're all parishioners. We didn't break in, we didn't break anything. We were even quiet. As a matter of fact, we kept all the empties in the boxes, so we didn't even litter".

That's when Joe farted.

The man who was stretched out over everyone's lap had a sudden attack of gas. Actually, with Joe, it was usually more like an attack WITH gas. An extremely noxious gas attack. And according to the attackees, it was an extremely vile chemical salvo that would have impressed even the World War I German High Command.

When the volcano of atmospheric distress started to erupt, the back seat occupants commenced with the coughing, retching, etc. Jerry, I think, had the sidewalk door, and he quickly tried to open the door so Joe could be summarily ejected. Police Car, the back doors don't open from the inside. So he quickly rolled down the window. (Remember, manually in those days.) Inconsolable Chris was at the other window, so they all started screaming for Chris to open the window.

"I'm dead. I'm friggan' dead."

Thus, the "Shut up" outburst.

This story does have a happy ending, though.

The police came up with a plan that would have made Solomon proud. They drove to the Rectory two blocks away on Brooklyn Ave to ask the Pastor what he wanted them to do with these trespassing parishioners. Apparently, he either recognized the names well enough to dismiss them with a warning or he didn't want to deal with the problem at that late hour. Whatever the reason, the cops happily let them all go. Telling them to go straight home with a statement that would become pretty familiar over the next few years:

"Don't let me see you again tonight."

Besides, Joe had already handed out a pretty mean punishment, as the cops found out when they got into the car to drive to the Rectory. A fate they didn't deserve. They had risen to the occasion. They relied on common sense and instinct to both protect and serve the community that helped infuse that common sense and instinct. They recognized these kids as part of the strength of the community and not a threat. Much to their credit.

So,

Chris did survive.

Most of them did get to Michaels. (I think Chris did follow the cops' directive and went straight home.)

Plus, I had won my argument with Phil. I had been rewarded for my courage to resist succumbing to his arguments.

How was I rewarded?

You see, if I had stayed ten seconds longer, had I not responded to that compelling voice of my upbringing, I would have been in that car. I also would have suffered through that gas attack. (Probably blinded by it, because, more than likely, I would have probably been laying on the six laps right next to Joe R.)

And, most probably mumbling along in chorus with Chris.

PART III - JUSTICE

I do believe that the most important of the five traits of an excellent community is justice. Justice ensures that all will get an equal chance at success. Please forget any image you may have gotten of lawyers, judges and court proceedings. The roles of those instruments of society is to protect the power structure. Their goal is to be punitive and their effect is to invoke limitations.

The definition of justice that contributes to excellence focuses on members getting what they earn. Not a penny less: and what may be more important, not a penny more. It is through this idea that we will get what we earn that accelerates the motor of a community toward excellence.

How so?

If we feel that each will eventually get what we earn, justice, we will work to our best abilities. Energetically put ourselves on the line for just rewards. No more than I deserve, but no less either. But the community has the responsibility to its members to provide for this. If our friends and family are going to have the courage to go forth and accomplish, then we owe it to them, and to us all, to work to make sure they don't get a raw deal.

But, if our just rewards have been gobbled up by a few greedy people, then too many neighbors will feel that expending their courage to follow their paths to success will not be worth the effort. This makes greed, the desire for something that we haven't earned, the malignant tumor of a Community of Excellent

THE SLAP OF JUSTICE

The primary source for my idea of how justice is defined is my father. He was able to explain this concept magnificently with a story about him and my grandfather. The story involves two slapping incidents with my grandfather, Thomas P. delivering the slaps and my father, Thomas F. delivering the lesson in justice.

There were two facts in this story really made me sit up and take notice when I heard them. The first, that my grandfather could be so out of character from my memory of him as to slap his son across the face, and the second, that he did this in front of witnesses.

As vague as my memory of my grandfather is, I do remember that when we would visit my grandparents all awe and fear any of us might have felt was reserved for my grandmother, Beatrice Harwood, nee Dillon, very affectionately known to her grandchildren as Lolla. She was a petite pepperpot of energy, discipline and hard work, all aimed at those she loved. My grandmother really was great to be with, as long as you didn't break any rules. My grandfather, Poppa, was more reserved, dignified and gentle. My memory of him is a man with a deep, intelligent gleam in a pair of eyes framed by wire rimmed glasses that were solidly perched a few inches above a warm smile. Thomas P. died when he was 83 and I was seven, so as I said, my memory of him is fairly vague. That being said, I was still having trouble picturing that dignified gentleman in that chair getting mad enough to slap anyone.

Let alone in public.

Part of that difficulty probably arises from the fact that my father was pretty good at avoiding administering his corporal punishments in front of audiences, especially non-family. But this story centers on him receiving a couple of public doses from his father.

The first incident occurred when Thomas F. was about 7 or 8 years old. That would be in 1931 or so, the depths of the Depression. He was entering his apartment building on the Upper East Side of Manhattan with Thomas P. when the superintendent confronted them to accuse young Tom of breaking a window while playing ball, and he expected that my grandfather would have to pay for it. Times being tough, I guess he felt some extra pressure, he exploded and slapped my father across the face. No questions asked and never giving his son a chance to respond.

The second incident happened in the principal's office at Power Memorial High School near the end of my father's senior year. The principal had called them there together to report that young Tom had cut one of his classes. The elder Tom again exploded and slapped his son in the face.

On the way home from the school, my grandfather was very upset that he had embarrassed his eighteen-year-old son and himself like that and tried to apologize.

Indignantly, my father broke in: "Don't apologize for that! I earned that! I cut that class! Apologize for slapping me in front of the building super with the broken window when I was seven. I was innocent then and didn't deserve that!"

The maturity of the victim and 10 years elapsed time could not overcome the pure conviction about justice that my father so deeply felt. This conviction was passed on so that all of his nine children adopted the same attitude toward justice. But, by the unanimous vote of the 7 other attendees to my father sharing this story, and later sustained by the rest of my extended family, I was selected as the primary heir to my father's level of conviction to this concept of justice. One of the greatest compliments I have ever received in my life.

Getting what you earn became a mainstay in everything I do. How I work. How I play. Who are friends. Who are not. This idea of justice is the basis for all that I consider moral and ethical.

Does the Car Feel Funny to You?

To the right of Chris in the cover picture comes Joey D. Sort of in the back. This is kind of appropriate because most of the time Joey sort of stayed to the rear. But he was always very diligent about being on his own correct path. Sometimes this took him to other places. Some other neighborhoods. Some other towns. But he belongs right there, part of the mix.

Joey is very smart. He's a mechanical engineer; a very talented engineer who is currently the Chief Engineer of an aeronautics company. But he did have a hint of the distracted genius element about him.

One morning he and I were commuting to Manhattan for work on a subway that crossed the East River via the Manhattan Bridge. The first time you take this subway line you become very impressed with the phenomenal view you get of Lower Manhattan, the Statue of Liberty and most of all, the Brooklyn Bridge located only a few hundred yards south. Daily commuters quickly put this excitement behind the morning paper, a good novel and sometimes heavy eyelids. On this trip, our fellow passengers overheard something to startle them into paying much closer attention.

In 1986, the year of this shared commute, the Brooklyn Bridge celebrated its 100th Anniversary and to advertise the upcoming gala the City of New York put posters all over the city, including in every single subway car. The poster's main attraction was the architect's original plan drawing showing the brand new bridge with its solidly reassuring stone towers and gracefully arching roadbed being supported by its intricate web of steel cables. I asked Joey if he understood what caused the obvious sagging in the roadbed that was very evident when you compared the actual century old bridge to the poster's rendering.

"Cable fatigue." He answered, matter-of-factly, and hardly diverting his attention from his book.

"Cable fatigue, what's that?" I asked, feigning ignorance of a concept that I actually learned about during my time at Brooklyn Technical High School.

Lifting his head and pointing out the obvious differences between the drawing and reality, he answered, "You see how the road bed flattens at the towers? That's because its weight has stretched the cables holding it up to greater lengths than originally designed. Over the 100 years, the stretch has gotten so bad that the road has sunk enough to settle onto the towers. Just like when you pull on a rubber band. Which means that they should be replaced before they snap."

"You mean that's happening to this bridge too? It's, what, maybe 7 or 8 years younger than the Brooklyn Bridge, right?" I asked, fully expecting the answer I got.

"Exactly like this bridge. Actually, no, this bridge would be worse because of the extra vibrations from the subway cars."

Joey went happily back to his book while I just stood there and enjoyed the growing number of sideways glances and concerned stares of the other riders who all seemed to be trying, albeit unsuccessfully, to sit as lightly and as still as they could and not add to the vibrations.

As entertaining as his Joey's absent-minded professor act can be, this a story about how he stayed very in tune with that most Flatbush of credos: 'Do the right thing, cause payback is a bitch.'

One night about seven years earlier, the six of us piled into Phil's car to go on one of our favorite road trips to Kennedy's Pier in Breezy Point. This was a place where we could meet up with some friends from Flatbush who summered down by the beach at Breezy Point. Also, we assumed that at least one of us would probably run into a rarely seen friend from school or who was also out for a nice summer night road trip.

Our fun evening there at an end, we decided to return to the car for the drive back to Mahoney's to close out the night. Upon arriving at Phil's Mercury Montego nicknamed the 'White

Knight', we find that we have a slight problem. Phil DOES indeed have a flat tire, but, not surprisingly, he DOESN'T have a spare.

Now what?

Two solutions were offered. Joey's; go back into Kennedy's and get someone to give us a ride to get another car and bring back a spare. Phil's; switch his flat with a good tire from some other car parked in the lot. Joey's was the right thing to do. Phil's was expedient. Right thing lost 4 votes to 2, Joey and I dissenting. The rest thought it would be okay if they took the tire from a new car, which was sure to have a spare.

In protest, Joey and I refused to help.

But once they located a new car with the right sized tire, they were having a lot of trouble trying to figure out how to move two tires with only one jack. The engineer instincts in Joey kicked in.

"I don't want them to damage someone else's car." Was his properly felt defense to me for countermanding our avowed nonparticipation. He demanded that they follow his instructions to the letter. They all agreed.

First, he insisted the tire had to come from the same spot on the victim car as Phil's flat; the passenger side rear tire. Next, he got us to move a railroad tie, which was moonlighting as a parking spot border, under Phil's car as they switched the tires on the poor innocent bystander car. While the others completed installing the stolen tire on the White Knight, Joey D and I turned our backs on their efforts to correctly replace the borrowed railroad tie to its proper original location. In a few minutes we were again on the road headed for home.

About 5 minutes into the ride I leaned forward and asked Joey, "Does the car feel funny to you?" We were both sitting on the right side of the car, he in the front seat riding 'shotgun' and me right behind him, and directly above the 'new' wheel.

"Yeah." Joey said. He turned to Phil and asked. "You sure you got the right size tire?"

"Yeah, yeah, perfect. Nothing to worry about. It's just fine." Phil countered impatiently.

General agreement and support for Phil so Joey and I let it drop, but only for a couple of more miles. He and I kept exchanging glances as we felt something wrong with the ride. I was told to shut up and that I was crazy the two other times I tried to raise the subject.

But then we got on the Marine Park Bridge and its metal roadbed.

"Whoa!!!!" Cried everyone in chorus. "Slow down Phil. There is something wrong." Now the glances Joey and I exchanged had a sense of triumph and vindication.

Theories abounded on what could be wrong as we slowly drove for the three minutes or so to clear the Bridge. "Air in the tire? Check. Are all the lug nuts tightened correctly? Check. Right size tire? Double check. All of us were at a loss at what could be wrong, even our resident engineer, Joey.

After clearing the tollbooth, we pulled over in front of the entrance to Floyd Bennett Field Air National Guard Base. Joey D and I were the first to hop out of the car, the first to examine the tire, and the first to fall on our backs laughing. Actually we were the only ones to fall down laughing. The others were just sort of standing around, giggling sheepishly and scraping at the ground with their toes.

The tire was installed inside out.

Instead of the wheel rim covering the brake drum and completely covered by the wheel well, it was put on so that about half of the tread width of the tire was sticking out from under the fender. This prevented the wheel from 'seating' securely to the axle and created the extra bounce that kept annoying Joey and me.

This time the two of us got a chance to sit comfortably on the grass and watch the Keystone Kop performance that our four friends gave us as they comically went about the business of correctly installing the stolen tire.

Poetic justice.

THE HIT

My favorite sport was, still is and will forever remain, hockey. Ice hockey, roller hockey, Rocky Hockey (on foot at St. Brendan's H.S. gym with basketball players). It didn't matter. The best time I could have was to play hockey from dawn til dusk (or dusk til dawn). One problem us New York City hockey players had to deal with, though, was that there's not much ice in the five boroughs.

In Brooklyn we had one indoor arena, Abe Stark in Coney Island. This was available for year round play and it was only about 45 minutes away by bus but we never went there because the neighborhood was pretty bad. Outdoors, there was Prospect Park. Not much organized hockey there, the rink was oddly shaped and only available in winter. Also, playing ice hockey was expensive and usually occurred in off hours, between 11:00pm to 6:00am. This made playing ice hockey very rare until we got old enough to drive.

The next best thing to ice hockey is roller hockey. DO NOT say street hockey. Real hockey, with a puck, no ball. I hate hockey with a ball.

Hockey in Brooklyn, and New York as a whole, was played by a pretty small community, once you got to a certain talent level. You got to know a lot of other players. Teammates on roller skates could sometimes be competitors on ice, and vice versa. Most of us became players on either the City of New York's Fire Department, Police Department or the Sanitation Department ice hockey teams in a local Industrial League. In fact, the fiercely contested annual Fire Dept./Police Dept. Game has been held in front of a sellout crowd at Madison Square Garden on a number of occasions.

The level of play in our roller hockey league was really pretty good. There were a lot of really good hockey players in Brooklyn at this time. The best from my part of town was John Borgia. He was about 5 years older than me and led the way for most of the other good players from the neighborhood. In Flatbush, you either learned the game from John, or from someone else who had learned the game from John. We were on a team together in a 15 – 17 year old league when I was 13 and he was 18. He was a small guy with a huge heart, huge mean streak and even huger shot. He taught me that you could play the game in a nasty mood and still maintain respect for your opponents and so earn their respect. This is a story about playing with respect; giving it and receiving it.

The league I played most of my games in was the Fort Hamilton Parkway Roller Hockey League. A rink, with boards, high intensity lights for night games, professional nets and an electric scoreboard was built in the park on 53rd Street and

Fort Hamilton Parkway in Bay Ridge section of Brooklyn mostly due to the efforts of the parkie there, Ray Miller. And the list of great players that played here is long. From Flatbush we had Tommy (Dusty) Beull, Joey Martin, Jimmy McMorrow, John Arnold, Smitty, Mackie, and quite a few others too numerous to name. From other parts of New York were Seppi, Billy Beggi, Mike Ryan (the best of all of us, in my opinion) and countless others whose names I can't remember.

As much as we shared a love and talent for this great game, we were all pretenders, enjoying our Sunday afternoons and Tuesday nights careening around some park at the northern edge of the Chassid part of Bay Ridge.

But there always was one of the New York hockey community who didn't pretend. He was the real deal. A legend. He made the jump from Chicago roller skates to lacing up his CCM Tacks in the NHL. He's arguably the best American born hockey player to date. And he's probably headed for the Hall of Fame.

Joey Mullin.

Joey had three brothers. Younger was Brian, who had a solid, if not as spectacular, career in the NHL. Older were Kevin and Tommy. They both played against me on a team called the Rockets at FHPRHL. My opinion about Mike Ryan notwithstanding, Tommy Mullin was the class of our league.

Tommy was always confronted with stupid questions about his brother, The Legend. Especially about Joe's opting off the Gold Medal 1980 Olympic Team to turn pro. He played the part of Legend's brother without even a hint of impatience for the questioner or bitterness with the questions. He was also a very talented player who didn't get a shot at the big time. Most probably because of his age. In spite of this, he always handled himself with class and respect. He showed me this personally one night and I've become a huge, life-long fan of his since. Let me tell you about it.

Tommy and most of his teammates were from the Hell's Kitchen section of Manhattan. They had basically two types of players, very talented or very bruising. Hell's Kitchen holds a backseat to no section of New York for toughness. And with the Mullin brothers leading the way, a lot of talented athletes from there got hooked on hockey.

In fact, I developed a pretty good on-ice* friendship with one of them. We were both about the same size, played the game pretty much the same way, we even wore the same number, 8. But I was blond, blue-eyed and only needed to shave every other day. He had dark, brown eyes and full beard. He looked so much like Stuart Margolin's character on 'The Rockford Files' that we all called him "Angel". *(Please note: even though we played on asphalt in a park, when playing you were said to be on-ice. Waiting to play, off-ice).

Angel and Tommy seemed to be really close friends. They arrived and left together. Spent warm-ups together. They even seemed to have a silent on-ice communication system. I started picking up on it because I was more of a defensive specialist who was constantly looking for things that would gain me some small edge against more talented players. If I could anticipate what they were going to do, it would help me when trying to guard against their playmaking.

Edge or not, Tommy's collection of interesting talents made him one of the most difficult players to shut down. He wasn't fast, but I never beat him to a loose puck or caught him from behind. He was a few pounds overweight, but very rarely was he caught out of position or taken out with a solid hit. His stickhandling was understated and subtle, but good luck trying to steal a puck from him. His point shot was only a quick wrist shot with hardly any backswing. But, it was rarely blocked and almost always 3 to 6 inches off the ground and ticketed for the far post. About as good as it gets. He wasn't a very aggressive player, but he was never pushed around. In fact, the one time I succeeded in getting a pretty good hit on him, I did more damage to myself. And I could throw a good hit.

This story actually concerns my hitting ability.

Hits, or body checks were an important part of my game. I was good at it and I shared this goodness as frequently as possible. I kept them clean: elbows and sticks down and never leaving my feet.

My offensive skills were of a supportive rather than finishing nature. I won face-offs, got the puck out of the corners, was immovable in front of the net and I could pass. My shot was, er.. Well, let's just say I always, ALWAYS, led the league in hitting the post. In fact, I was famous for hitting the post as I was for my hits.

So the perfect line mates for me would be finishers or shooters. Beech, my right wing, was the finisher, John, on the left, had the shot. Actually, John had a big shot. One of the hardest in the league. But, it took him a long time to get it off.

How long?

Long enough for the goalie to send out for pizza and check tomorrow's weather between set-up and save. So, if we were going to take advantage of John's shot, we needed a play.

It was a 3-on-2 or 3-on-3 play. We needed the three of us to break out of our own zone together. Beech and I steaming up the right wing, exchanging passes when necessary, John lumbering up the left wing trying to be invisible. About two strides before their blue line, Beech and I would break suddenly to the left. Me with the puck, him to stay on side. Once I cleared the blue line Beech would cut back to the boards and slowly approach the net from the wing. I would fake that I was going up the middle and again cut left, as if to go wide on the defenseman. But at a point about four feet inside the zone and twice as far from the left wing sideboards, I would drop the puck, leave it still and flat. John would already be winding up. As John shot, I would be skating right at the defenseman toward the net.

33% of the time we ran this play, the shot went wide right. Beech being in a good spot to retrieve it. 33% of the time, the shot would either hit my unprotected calf (ouch!) or the padded shin of the defenseman. 33% of the time the shot was on net. In about 4 years together, I think we scored twice. We liked the play anyway. It gave John something to do.

Early in the third period of a game against the Rockets, we broke out on a 3 on 2. Beech, John and I facing two of their defensemen. We were losing badly, the score at this point was probably Rockets-7 or 8 to Blues-1.

The left defenseman, facing Beech, was a tall, slim, blond, bearded, talented defenseman. The other one was a bruiser, maybe THE bruiser. A very goonish 6ft 1in, 225 – 230lb linebacker of a man with the commensurate mean and nasty disposition. This actually worked to our favor because he was the one who had to display some hockey instinct to stop our play. So I streaked at him to make him start retreating deep in his zone. I never counted on him be so uninstinctive that he would not cross over to skate backwards but just sweep his stick at mine and unexpectedly succeed at knocking the puck to the left wing boards. End of play?

Not hardly.

Beech was still one on one in front and John would set-up in the high slot (in the center of the zone closer to the blue line than the net). So if I could retrieve the puck first, we still had a chance for a shot and a good scoring chance.

Not to be.

The Big Bruising Defenseman (BBD for the rest of this story) never even looked at the puck as I was doing. At least, I was looking at the puck for a couple of seconds. Then I saw stars. BBD was more intent on smashing me through the boards than retrieving the loose puck. I had never been hit that hard in my life and fell crashing and spinning to the ground. After the moment it took to stop my head from swirling, I saw BBD trying to settle the hard to control, bouncing puck about 6 feet in front of me. By the time it took for him to get possession of the puck and look for a play, I was up, muscling my way between him and the boards, lifting his stick with mine and kicking the puck toward the corner. We now had another race for the loose puck.

I got there first, he got there a second later. SMASH. Huge hit number 2 in less than 5 seconds. Hit number 2 was actually hits numbers 2, 3 and 4. He caught up to me as the side boards angled (not arced) to the end boards. It was here that they decided to put a gate. A very bouncy double gate. After hit 1, I bounced off gate 1 and back to BBD, who slammed me into gate 2 where I bounced back to BBD, who slammed me into the end boards where there was no bounce. Lots of pain and lots more stars. Up until this point in my life, it was the second hardest hit I had ever received. Hit 1 had been the hardest.

Seeing his partner "take the man", Bearded Talented Defenseman (BTD for the rest of this story) went to back up his teammate by going for the puck. (A good question now is why had not my teammates come to help me? Answer, I didn't need it. Remember I said I get the puck, they shoot? Well, I got up and got the puck. BBD and BTD were locked in a classic "You? or Me?" paralysis. I just stepped between them and tried to pass in front to a wide-open Beech.

Three things then happened almost simultaneously.

1. Their goalie blocked my pass and dumped puck behind the net.
2. BTD skated behind the net to retrieve the puck and start stick handling toward the far corner.
3. I started counting more constellations.

BBD had had enough. Now he was really mad. This time he hit me really hard. This was quickly becoming a bad habit. I was strongly hoping for my 'Hardest-Hit-Received' record to last, maybe ten, twenty years or so. But no, not even 5 more seconds.

As I rolled over and got back to my feet, my linemates were hustling to keep the pressure on. Beech had successfully cut BTD off near the corner. As those two were fighting for the puck, John had moved over to the boards to intercept any clearing attempt that way. I needed to get to that high slot as quickly as I could to cover for them.

I went forthwith. Well, I paused a second to give BBD a small poke of protest in the back of the leg as I went by. A way of saying 'you got me that time, but I'll be back'. He offered me a 'you're welcome' poke to my leg in response.

I actually went out higher than the slot. I didn't intend to turn until I reached the blue line. It was on my mind to get ready to change for a fresh line, I needed a rest from the Astronomy lessons that BBD was giving me. I was waiting to make sure it was safe for me to start the change.

But then he did it. BBD lost his respect for us. He insulted my team and me. He got cocky. Now it was my turn to get mad. I had had enough.

When you're winning 7 to 1 you get conservative. If you have any respect for your opponents, you don't do anything to show them up. You play hard, traditional, keep them down hockey. Meaning that if your partner's breakout is cut off in the left corner and no one is pressuring your goaltender, you spread out and be an outlet in the right corner. But BBD had a different idea. He broke out up the slot.

He had no business taking that kind of risk. By doing it he was telling us we couldn't do anything about it. This was insulting, but not so bad that I would lose my temper because of it.

But BBD didn't stop there. He took his insulting behavior to another level, an entirely unacceptable level.

He started slapping his stick blade on the ice calling for the puck. This was outrageous. This was something you do in the offensive zone when you're in position to score. He had over 100 feet to go.

I got pissed and, tired or not, aching or not, I intended to do something about this.

I started watching BTD waiting for his legs to move under him for balance to make his pass. When they did, I made a quick 180 degree turn, and raced straight at the 6ft 1in 225lb BBD as fast as my 5ft 9in, 180lb body could go.

Yeah, yeah, I know, he had the size advantage. But I never in my whole life, ever, EVER, let something like a size disadvantage stop me. I'd never do anything. They were always bigger than me! In fact, the fact that he was bigger got me even more pissed.

To my advantage in this impending confrontation was surprise, timing, speed, good looks, superior intelligence, adrenalin enhanced rage and, most importantly, a lower center of gravity. I decided to improve this with a Ronnie Forearm.

Ronnie was a defensive back in our bar football league, and like me, he was no giant. He taught me that if you can get your forearm under a taller guy's ribs, you raised him off his feet a little and added to that center of gravity thing.

It was time to test his theory.

The timing of the hit was absolutely perfect. BBD was just looking up after gaining possession of BTD's pass as I lit into him. Forearm properly placed under his ribs, I followed through by driving my right shoulder into his solar plexus precipitating a collision of seismic proportions. This time, I didn't see stars, I saw whole galaxies. The collision must have looked great. I, however, couldn't see too much. My head was spinning and my eyes were tearing. My forearm throbbed from being crushed between us and every bone, ligament, cartilage, fiber, atom, in my body screamed in agony. I had also blasted out about 95% of the air in my lungs.

But I smiled anyway. I had to put my stick down in front of me so I wouldn't fall. I decided that there was no amount of pain, loss of oxygen, ringing in my ears or flashing lights in my head that would make me fall down.

After a second to get my bearings and my vision to clear a little, I could see BBD, who an instant before had made one of the most delightful groaning sounds I have ever heard, then or since, lying on his back holding his head with his bare hands. His stick had landed about 15 feet behind me and each glove had bounced similar distances on either flank. A beautiful sight. At least as much as I could make out through my blurry vision.

Whoa, whoa, now wait a minute. I did say this was a Tommy Mullin classy story, didn't I. Well, it is.

As I collected my bearings and turned to struggle to my bench about 50 feet behind me to the right, I stopped to focus on one of the best compliments of my life. Tommy and Angel were leaning out of their bench and banging their sticks against the boards. Hockey applause. Two players on the other team just watched me take 5 huge hits along the boards from their most bruising player and then turn around and return the favor with an even bigger open-ice hit. And they were giving me a standing ovation for it!!!

I smiled again.

But that smile didn't have long to live. We still lost 8 −1. At the end of the game I was uncharacteristically quick about congratulating their goalie and a few of their players for a good game and slumped off to get changed. This was NOT a good game. I hated to lose, even if by one goal. But by 7. This was a rout that would make me an unsociable grouch for at least a half hour.

At Ft Hamilton, each team had its own 'locker room', certain benches in the park that were used for donning and removing your equipment. The Blues changed on the benches that surrounded the kiddie sprinkler on the Ft Hamilton Ave. side of the park. I usually sat near one of the bench turns in the middle of my team. But when we lost like this, and looking to cool down a little by myself, I would move down the bench beyond the end of the sprinklers, closer to the swings. This seat looked directly toward the basketball courts on the far side of the park away from Ft Hamilton Parkway, which was where the Rockets changed.

As is usual with hockey players, I had a ritual for dressing and undressing for a game. After having removed my helmet, gloves, shirt, and elbow pads, I bent down to unlace both my skates. As I sat up from getting the left skate off, I stopped short. Coming right at me from the basketball court was Tommy Mullin and Angel. Each had an open can of beer in one hand with Tommy carrying the remaining 4 cans by an empty spot in the plastic rings.

Seating themselves on either side of me, Tommy said "Good game." But I was too stunned to answer.

"Head clear yet" asked Angel as he peered into my face. "Should I check for loose teeth?"

"How many fingers do you see?" Asked Tommy, who instead of holding up any fingers, was handing me the remnants of the six-pack for me to help myself to one. I just laughed. Of all the compliments I have ever received this one touched me right to my very soul. Any residual unsociable grouchiness disappeared before the top of my beer snapped open.

We drank those six beers and talked. I don't think we talked about the game, but we did spend time on hockey. I probably even had time enough for three stupid "Joey Mullin" questions, which Tommy handled with his usual class. They had come to show some respect to a fellow hockey player. They made me feel great, like a partner. They wanted me, and through me, my team, to know that BBD was wrong. That you don't show up your opponents as he had. Winning can be glorious, but only if you maintain your opponents dignity as well as your own. The more worthy the opponent, the more glorious the victory. Spit on your opponent, you spit on your own victory, cheapening it.

But they also had a message for their own team. Spit on your opponents, like BBD, and you run the risk of being an outcast. No one is greater than the team. No one is going to diminish their victories. The team will not tolerate it. If you go ahead and put yourself ahead of the team, they will put you back where you belong.

Everyone gets only what they earn.

M A R Q U I S

(P R O N O U N C E D M A R K U S)

Marquis was the funniest man in Brooklyn. He was also one of
the most liked. The kind of person that legends just seemed to
grow around.

He was the quickest on the draw with one-liners. But rarely
made anyone feel bad. This was because he had a smile 5 feet 6
inches tall and 175 pounds (statistics approximate) that always
went with anything he said. Also, he spread it around evenly.
There were a few of us that offered him better inspiration, but
he kept his attention pretty well balanced among everyone.
Marquis could take on four or five people in a rank out session
and leave them gasping for breath in less time than it takes to
drink a glass of beer.

There were two other outstanding characteristics about
Marquis. He was one of the longest lasting drinkers around and
he could be a bit of a philosopher.

Marquis was the drinking hero of the Snyder/Church Avenue contingent to Mahoney's. He was a happy man who got happier as he drank. Screwdrivers or beer being his preferred drinks. He was known in his circle to have a lot of stamina. His childhood friends bragged he could outlast any who tried him. He lost only once. Even though this wasn't an 'official' drinking contest with rules, referees and witnesses, it was a classic.

What made this a classic was his competition and the reaction of the competitor's friends as they awaited a decision. His adversary in this pseudo-contest was our guy, my man, Joe R. As good as Marquis was, I knew no one could compete with Joe when it came to partying. With one possible exception, I spent more nights out with him than anyone else. Joe, like Marquis, could last a long time when out drinking. His reputation for stamina gave rise to us developing theories to try to explain Joe's ability to drink for such a long period of time.

One theory held that he had to work so hard just to walk, er, limp, everywhere, that he limped himself sober. This relied on the fact that Joe had one leg shorter than the other from a broken hip when he was thirteen. But I didn't need a theory. I can tell everyone for a fact that there was another, truer reason. Joe could drink for long sessions because he was so involved in having fun that his adrenaline was always up. This meant he was always sweating the alcohol out of his system. He carried the nickname Pits for a few years because he once took off his coat after coming in out of the cold, 5 degrees over zero, with only a tee-shirt on underneath and had sweat rings under his arms that drooped halfway to his hips.

But this is a story about Marquis. Even though the victory would be Joe's, the story would be Marquis'. The event took place out at the Hamptons. The Hamptons has received notice as the summer playground of the rich and famous. But there is enough Hamptons to go around for everyone. Our sector centered on the Village of Hampton Bays, which sat about 5 miles west of the center of their beach resort, the Village of Southampton.

Joe and Marquis had met up one evening at the best party bar in Hampton Bays, The Bawdy Barn, and decided to travel around together for some fun. As I said, they weren't actually having a drinking contest, per se. They didn't drink the same stuff nor sit around with witnesses and judges. They just went out for some fun and circumstances put them together for a legendary night and then some.

That summer Joe and I were not staying with the rest of our friends. We had rented a house on the east side of the Hampton Bays. The rest of our crew had a cabin on the west side of the bay across the street from the Oak Tree Inn. On that momentous Saturday evening I showed up at the cabin and found the residents, Phil and Chris, plus some guests, Joey M and Frannie, Church/Snyder guys, all over each other because they heard that Marquis and Joe had gone off alone for happy hour. They were all talking up their favorite partyer as the one who would be the 'last man' standing. Money was being bet and tales of largess were being bragged about. Phil and Chris were getting pretty worked up about Joe being untouchable, granting that Marquis was legitimate competition. Even so, no sap from Church Ave could take down Joe R. The other two protested vehemently that Marquis was the king. Actually, only Frannie was Church Ave, Joey was from a more neutral address but he had seen Marquis overcome entire rooms. His main contact with Joe was as my great friend and an avid, but clumsy, hockey player. So he fell in for Marquis.

So, on that fine summer Saturday, the stage was set and the hunt was on. Dozens of people were interested in the outcome when word got around that Joe and Marquis had hooked up for happy hour and were out together to parts unknown. Anyone who knew them would understand the implications of this match-up, so the word got out quickly and report after report worked their way back to the cabin via the Oak Tree, all saying Joe and Marquis were nowhere to be found.

We went out that night, but never saw them. Nor did anyone else. This was pretty strange because neither Joe or Marquis drove, and traveling in the Hamptons was next to impossible without a car. As that night progressed, we still had no word. The suspense began to build as the night advanced into the prime hours, 11:30 PM - 4:00 AM, and still no sighting.

I went back to my house and slept well. I knew Joe was in control. I knew this because they were completely out of touch. It wasn't Marquis style to seek out new life and new civilizations, to boldly go where no party had gone before. But Joe was the best at this. I can't tell you how many times he and I would be walking somewhere when Joe would say he knew someone that hung out at a particular bar. Only to find out later that he just made that up to get me to go in. But, in spite of the deception, we always found new friends and we always had a great time.

I got back to the cabin the next morning about 11:00. Still no word yet, but the trash talking among the betting public was in high gear. A few more Flatbush citizens had come by so more bets were being made and some standing bets were being doubled. Money and reputations were on the line.

This was great. I was having a great time watching a group of very close friends ping-pong exaggerated claims that were quickly followed by more betting and more raises. The actual value of the betting was low, but the intensity was feverous.

I was pretty much left out of all this. Since Joe and I were so close and everyone knew I didn't bet, it didn't make any sense to go after me. But everyone else's expectations were building at a landslide pace.

The energy wasted on the claims and counter-claims finally seemed to burn the Monte Carlo madness down to nothing. After about an hour of intense exchanges we all seemed to need to find a calmer hiatus. I drifted down to the beach. Chris went for a shower. Phil went to the bar for ice while his lab assistants, Frannie and Joe M, were in the middle of a discussion on the best recipe for a vodka punch. In the midst of all this, Marquis struggled in. He stumbled through a gauntlet of mesmerized stares and got three steps inside the door before finally collapsing, without a word, on the couch. Question after question was fired at him but all we could get out of Marquis was a 'Ralph Kramden-like' wave that signified Joe R was still "out there, somewhere" as he fell into a deep sleep.

The two sides were now left to argue whether Marquis was the only one capable of getting home. One side proposing that he had left Joe sleeping it off under some tree or something. But I just laughed and said, "No way. Joe is still on his feet and going strong". I knew Marquis would never lose his friend's back. He would never leave Joe behind unless he knew that he was okay. Besides, I knew better than anyone what that look on Marquis' face meant. I had seen that same face in my mirror dozens of times. I knew Joe had won.

So why is this a story about Marquis. Because he handled this like the first class man he is. A couple of hours later, he roused just long enough to tell us what happened.

"That boy is amazing." he started. "We left the happy hour at The Bawdy Barn and started bar hopping. We would just walk until we came to a bar and in we'd go. Joe would just start hanging out with whoever was there. We're having a great time, and I thought we were done but then that guy then takes me into a party about five this morning. At somebody's house. He walks in and starts introducing me around to all these people, acting like he knew them. About 10:00 this morning somebody finally asked ME who JOE was. They said it was not a problem about us being there, since they were having a better time now than before, but they kinda like to know who we were and where we're from. I told them, waited about ten minutes, snuck out and walked back here." Marquis tapered off with that last sentence and started to fall back to sleep.

"But where's Joe?" I think Frannie asked.

"Still there. Man that boy can drink. Never saw anyone like him. S-o-n-o-f-a-bitch!"

Marquis knew that we were all sitting around waiting for the details and couldn't leave us hanging. But by offering the praise that Joe R had earned, he forced us to act a little better about things. We remembered that we work to make sure everyone gets what they deserve, good, as with Joe, and bad as with the co-star in the next story.

This was also a drinking contest and it was a great episode that illustrated Marquis' ability to phrase our philosophical priorities in a way that sticks with you. It was the only time I remember him ever getting nasty to somebody. And it is my single favorite story about my time hanging out at Mahoney's.

A group of my friends were settled into our office at the bar, under the television by the front window. Marquis, Mickey, me, and a few others. In walked somebody that both Mickey and Marquis recognized. Mickey smiled a warm greeting, Marquis did not.

Marquis was standing at the bar next to the wall. Mickey and the unknown Stranger were by the window using the cigarette machine for an end table. The Stranger was an obnoxious asshole. He was one of those people that barely needed thirty seconds to piss you off.

If I said I weighed 175 lbs, he weighed 176. If I could run the 100-yard dash in 11 seconds, he could do it in 10.5. He was constantly spewing one-ups on anything anyone had to say. His undoing finally came when he said something to the effect that he could out-drink anyone in the bar.

"You can out-drink me?!" Marquis screamed.

"Sure" said the Stranger. "No problem." This created a tense silence from all in attendance.

"That's it ass-hole. Twenty dollars says I can drink five beers faster than you can drink five shots of anything you want." said Marquis.

"You're on!" replied the Stranger.

"Okay, here's the rules. One, the bartender holds the money, he decides who wins. Two, the drink is not finished until the empty glass is on the bar. Three, you can't touch my glasses, I can't touch yours. Deal?" Marquis detailed.

"Done." Agreed the Stranger.

The crowd edged closer for a better view, but maintaining a good enough distance so as not to interfere as the bartender poured out the beers and the shots and laid them out at right angles to each other at the turn of the bar. Both combatants would be working from right to left. The Stranger moving from the middle of the bar to the corner. Marquis from the corner to the wall.

After putting their left hands in their back pockets, both drinkers leaned forward, hands at the ready around the first glass, waiting for the bartender to say go.

"Go!"

The first beer and shot went down like a flash. At almost the same instant Marquis and the Stranger slammed their empty glasses on the bar, the Stranger grabbed his second shot and fired it down like lightening. As he grabbed the third, he noticed that Marquis was leaning against the bar, smiling that 5 foot 6 inch smile of his and not drinking.

Not drinking?

Then the Stranger got it.

Marquis' first empty glass had been turned upside down and placed over the Stranger's last shot.

"Hey, that's bullspit." he lamented.

"Keep your hands off that glass." Said the bartender/referee. "You can't touch his glass, he can't touch yours."

"But he touched it!" weakly pleaded the Stranger as he searched one onlooker's face after another. Gone was all his bravado. Now a very desperate man was quickly trying to get a BIG foot out of his mouth. He started begging for some support from the crowd. Not a chance.

"Never did." said Marquis.

"I watched him. " confirmed the bartender.

The Stranger was sunk and he knew it. He started staring at his $40 problem first from the left, then from the right. He brought his eyes level with the bar top to get the front view. Then he tried stretching over the bar to get a look from behind. It got so bad that he even offered five dollars to the next person through the door to pick up the offending glass. The crowd would have none of it.

This was a fair contest, fairly agreed to and being fairly administered. And fairly screwing him out of $20. (Inflation being what it is, back then, that $20 could have purchased these two that round of 5 beers and 5 shots at least 3 more times.)

The fact that he was getting only what his big mouth had bought him only made his petty attempts to dig himself out of this, all the funnier. His unacceptable behavior even succeeded at turning his one ally, Mickey, against him.

Marquis decided to savor his victory and took an uncharacteristic 45 minutes to slowly drink the next three beers. All the while wearing a smile that seemed grow taller than the 5 foot 6 inches he was, and heartier than the 175 pounds he weighed.

THIS WAS GREAT!

When Marquis finally got to his fifth beer, he shared the moral for this fable. It's a great lesson. Spoken in a poetic style that only a Philosopher like Marquis could come up with, and then make sure those who heard it would always remember it and abide by it.

"IF YOU ACT LIKE AN ASS-HOLE, YOU GOTTA EXPECT
TO GET TREATED LIKE AN ASS-HOLE."

That last beer was downed in two seconds flat. The two twenties quickly disappeared into his pocket. With a wave to the crowd and a nod to the bartender, he was gone. But not before leaving behind a generous tip for the bartender/referee and the fading strains of one of our favorite Irish songs:

"With a shillelagh under me arm and a twinkle in me eye, I'm off to Tipperary in the morning...."

But the Light's Red

It was shaping up to be another nice autumn Saturday afternoon. What a wonderful day for a drive, she thought. Being the nice lady that she was, she probably wanted to go out and do a few chores or make a few friendly visits. "Let's go for a ride in the car today, Muffy!" She said to her bouncy, chipper mini poodle. "That should be nice, shouldn't it?"

It didn't quite turn out that way.

You see this Saturday afternoon the light on Albany Avenue and Avenue I was broken. Oddly, it was stuck on red for Albany Ave and green for Avenue I. I had always thought that when a traffic light breaks, it automatically starts blinking flashes of red (stop sign) for one road and yellow (proceed with caution) for the other. I guess the police had to dispatch a patrol car to do this manually once they got a report.

We ran into the broken light on the way to The White Horse. This was a private club for paying members and their friends that happened to sponsor the best football team in our bar league at this time. The club was on Ave J between Albany Av and E 42nd St. We had embarked on this trip from Mahoney's, which was six long city blocks away down Albany.

I'm not sure why we went there to begin with. White Horse was usually pretty dead on Saturday afternoons. Its hot time was after 4 am when the bars were forced to close by law but private clubs were allowed to stay open, but only to members and their guests. Regardless, we decided to take the drive, probably because it was such a nice day for a drive.

Phil, driving the 'White Knight', was accompanied by Pat, Peter and me. Pat riding shotgun in the front passenger seat manning the radio, Peter and I in back trying to keep our balance. We were having trouble because those wells in the floor that were normally reserved for feet were completely filled with empty beer bottles and cans. We were uncomfortably working our feet into spots on the hump in the middle and under the door that kept our feet out of the trash but didn't hurt your knees or ankles too much.

In spite of this discomfort, the drive was calm and soothingly distracting. Nothing too exciting. The conversations sedate. The jokes at a minimum. The music at a low volume. The only memorable event during our cruise to White Horse was the broken light. Phil, after waiting at least double the time generally expected for a red light cycle, proceeded as if at a stop sign. Just as he was supposed to.

After a short stay at White Horse, I guess we confirmed its Saturday afternoon reputation for boring, we decided to return to Mahoney's.

A decision that fate had put aside to ruin this wonderful afternoon for a nice old lady who just wanted to take a pleasant ride with her loving poodle. She was destined for a dose of aggravation that she was totally unprepared for and most assuredly didn't deserve.

And all she did was what she was supposed to do. Stop at a red light. And wait for it to change to green before proceeding. What went wrong was that we stopped behind her.

Phil gave a polite toot on his horn to get her attention, "Maam, the light's broken. You can go. It's just like a stop sign. Okay?" He called out as politely as anyone could.

What her reaction was to Phil's first attempt, we're not sure, but her mini poodle seemed to get pissed.

"YIP! YIP! YIP! YIP!" Piped the pipsqueak poodle as it bounced from side to side in the back seat. Jumping up and down on the back dash.

Phil's response? HONK. "Lady, you can go. The light's broken."

Then the argument commenced.

"YIP! YIP! YIP! YIP!" Bounce. Bounce. Bounce. Bounce.

HONK. "Lady, the light's broken. You can go!"

After about four repetitions of Phil losing his argument with a dog, Pat offered some mediation.

"Phil, why don't you just back up and go around her?"

HONK! "Lady, the light's broken. You can go."

"YIP! YIP! YIP! YIP!" Bounce. Bounce. Bounce. Bounce.

"Come on Phil. Go around her." I seconded Pat's common sense.

HONK! "Lady, the light's broken. You can go."

"YIP! YIP! YIP! YIP!" Bounce. Bounce. Bounce. Bounce.

Peter then tried. But there was no weakening in the resolve of Phil, or the poodle for that matter, to win this confrontation and convince his adversary he was right. The poodle seemed to be getting frustrated that Phil wasn't getting his point. The more he YIPped and bounced the more Phil HONKed and called out for the wonderful lady that was its mistress to move through a red light.

Phil also got frustrated. He realized he needed to do something to snap this woman out of her paralysis. He elevated the incident by slowly, V-E-R-Y slowly rolling up on the rear bumper of her car, and then nudged it.

Quick as a flash the tail lights flash indicating the car was being put in park. The door bursts open.

The poodle intensified its YIPped support as its mistress emerged from the car struggling to maintain her normally vast amount of dignity despite her growing rage at this lunatic behind her. She looked very much like a first grade teacher or a lady at the reference desk at the library.

"What's your problem! Can't you see the light's red?!" said the obviously nice lady who had been driven to an unfamiliar and uncomfortable aggravation level. I got the impression that this was the loudest she had ever spoken in her entire life.

"Lady, the light's broken. You can go through it. We saw it on the way down here." Phil explained.

"YIP! YIP! YIP! YIP!" Bounce. Bounce. Bounce. Bounce.

"What's wrong with you? You hit my car!" She said as she stepped toward the rear of her car to check for damage.

"Excuse me, lady, are you going to move your car?"

"YIP! YIP! YIP! YIP!" Bounce. Bounce. Bounce. Bounce.

"NO! I'm going to wait for the light to turn green. Can't you see the red light?"

"Are you going to move your car?" Phil's head slumped down onto his right hand.

"YIP! YIP! YIP! YIP!" Bounce. Bounce. Bounce. Bounce

The three-part argument repeated itself a couple of more times. Pat looked back at us with an expression that probably mirrored the discomfort and embarrassment Peter and I were feeling. We didn't like Phil giving this nice little old lady such a hard time. But the dog was definitely becoming as pleasant as a leaky faucet at three A.M. Apparently, this was bothering Phil too.

His left hand went up. "Lady, please stop." He began. His next sentence came out slow and clear. Each word painfully enunciated and exaggeratedly spaced. "Are...you...going... to...move...your...car?"

"YIP! YIP! YIP! YIP!" Bounce. Bounce. Bounce. Bounce

"It's a red li...."

"Okay!" The White Knight goes into park. Phil's head slowly lifts off his palm and turns until he is staring full face at this chocolate chip cookie baking grandmother look-alike.

"That's it! We're going to kill your dog!"

Absolute silence. The lady's jaw dropped. Our jaws dropped. The poodle's jaw dropped. It even disenYIPped and disenbounced. As a matter of fact, there wasn't a sound to be heard at all.

This poor, lovely woman, minding her own business, out for a pleasant drive on a beautiful autumn afternoon, with her beloved mini poodle, went into shock. Her gaze transfixed on Phil's 'What are you going to do now' expression.

With a slow shaking of her head, she hesitantly turned toward her car. Her first step slow and deliberate but her pace increased to 'sub-frenzy' with each subsequent step as she rushed back to her car, put it in gear, and moved over as far right as she could without entering the intersection too much.

Phil put his car in gear, spun the wheel left, rolled to the intersection. Came to a full stop. Looked both ways. And took off.

"Hey, Phil. What would you say if I told you there was a cop car parked right there on Avenue I?" I asked.

"Bullspit, Richie. That's not funny." Phil responded to the laughter my question got out of Pat and Peter. The three of us were not feeling to good about what Phil just did to that lady, so we were especially vulnerable to some comedy right then.

"It's also not bullspit. I saw them there." I insisted. "But, I don't think they saw anything. Or they don't care because they're not coming."

"Richie, your full of ..." Phil stuttered to a stop mid-sentence. This wasn't because he had to stop at the red light at Avenue H, but because he saw a police car in the mirror advancing quickly up Albany Avenue with lights flashing but with its siren silent.

The light turns green and Phil starts to go. Now the siren sounds. Phil pulls over to the curb on the trestle over the LIRR freight train tracks.

"What the hell was that?" Demanded cop A as he rushed to Phil's window. I don't think that that was normal police procedure, but this could hardly be considered a normal situation

"Look Officer, " Phil explained. "The light was broken; I told her the light was broken. I asked her to move the car. But she wouldn't move the car. I asked and I asked. But she still wouldn't move. I was being really nice. But she wouldn't move. So I told her I was going to kill her dog. So she moved."

The truth, the whole truth, nothing but the truth, so help me God.

During this exchange, Pat was unsuccessfully trying to snort down his growing laughter. Peter and I couldn't laugh because we were too busy trying to sit with our knees uncomfortably together to hide the piles of empties at our feet.

Even though his partner's behavior might be a step off, the other Policeman was following procedures to the letter. He moved to the passenger side of the car and stopped at a point even with the front door to keep his eye on the passengers while his partner took care of the driver. One look at Pat's face and he could see we weren't a threat. One look at Peter's and he could see the incident was over. Peter waved and nodded to confirm the recognition.

"Jack, let's go. Let it drop." He told his partner.

"What? ..." He cut himself off when he saw the look on his partner's face. Peter's father was one of the many fathers in our neighborhood who had attained high rank in the Police Department.

Officer A finished with the expected "I don't want to see you again today, clear?"

"Yes sir, officer. You won't. Thank you." Phil answered.

Now, upon review, we can't really get emotionally indignant about Phil's behavior. He followed the code, almost. The abuse of the old lady and the bumping of her car were wrong. But he could never really have done anything to harm her. He had to do something. His instincts for confronting the problem were blazing for action. And that dog was a huge pain in the ass. The threat on the dog was definitely empty.

Besides, he was honest and respectful to the police. We all knew that you acted in the appropriate fashion with the police. They earn our respect every day. They deserve to be treated correctly. They could be relied upon to do the right thing, so long as you didn't do anything to make them feel angry or threatened. Peter's father notwithstanding, we probably would have gotten the same response from the cops as we did, though there would have been a longer discussion.

If you do feel that the scales of justice owe Phil something for his behavior, rest assured. Justice never sleeps. It might take a patient approach but it will win out in time. We can expect to get what we earn.

Phil's justice? Well. The next time you see Phil ask him "How's Buddy?" That way he'll tell you all about his cute little, bouncy, yippy thing of a mini poodle.

PART IV - TOLERANCE

My specific definition of tolerance focuses on each of us supporting our neighbors right to define themselves as they see fit. Our community needs each of us to give our best, our particular talents and our unique outlook. To do that, we must not try to fit ourselves into someone else's categorization but establish our own personality for ourselves. It is not so important how others see you but how you see yourself. Fellow community members who support and encourage this individuality are activating whatever personal talent, genius or viewpoint that each of us can offer. And this leads to energetic innovation.

If we are tolerant of others, we include them. The more people pulling on the oars the faster we go. The more people involved on a problem, the better chance of a new look, or a different idea that can offer a unique solution. Building a team can lead to an unexpected way of doing something or adding new information to the mix. Mixing these ideas with other new ideas, and some old ideas as well. All members being exposed to all ideas because all are included. There is no way to anticipate what contribution tomorrow's problems may require, there's no way to anticipate who can or will stand up and take care of those unforeseen problems. Inclusion is power. Exclusion is suicide.

Tolerance ensures that the excellence we seek as a community can grow to unanticipated heights.

BEING A BIG BROTHER

Unfortunately, when I looked back for stories about tolerance, there are far more examples of failure in this regard than success. This is the hard one. This is the trait that is hardest to define, hardest to understand and hardest to implement. But as with most difficult tasks, this is the one that reaps the most benefit and the most gratification. Most of the stories in this section will point out incidents of failed tolerance, and I start with myself.

I've offered some history about two of my older siblings, but the next in line after Tommy and Madelyn, comes Bobby. When I talk about Bobby I'm talking about not just a great brother, he was a great friend, too. We were close growing up. Which is more to his credit than mine. Younger brothers, as I was, two years different, are quite often looked on as a burden or a nuisance by most of us. But not to him. I can't remember a moment where he didn't let me tag along when he did things with his friends. Whether it was playing football or baseball or basketball. Going to someone's house to listen to music or look for galaxies through his telescope, I was always welcome.

Bobby and I shared countless trips to Mets and Yankee games, and to the Planetarium in Manhattan. I was constantly backstage at Lincoln Center when Bobby was singing as a youth in operas and musicals performed there. When he became the headline talent of our parish's teenagers theatrical group known as The Silver Masque Players, everyone knew that on July 29, 1969, the day after I turned 13, I was going to join even though my singing talent could only be used to clear a room in case of a fire. And to the credit of Mr. And Mrs. John Mallon, the Silver Masque directors, I was welcomed with open arms. I can't say we were constantly together, but we were together often enough that when something interesting to do came to either of us, we naturally assumed that we would include the other.

This was a lesson I definitely missed. It was a far cry from how I treated my younger brothers and sisters. With him as an example, I should have done a lot better for Kenny, Paul, Jimmy, Maryellen and Carolyn. Especially Kenny.

I can't say I took Kenny anywhere like this. In fact, the only time I can remember even sticking up for him was at a dental clinic when I threatened to attack the dentist who was causing him such obvious pain. It seemed to me that most of my interaction with Kenny resulted in me being reminded of the main sources of frustration I had with my life, especially how small I was, and then blaming him. Even though he was two years younger than me, he would get Bobby's cloths handed down to him before I did. This infuriated me, and even though it wasn't his fault, I took that fury out on him.

I consider this the single greatest failing in my life. Not just the specific treatment of Kenny, but also how I bullied my other younger brothers and sisters and ordered them around.

When I got old enough to realize my errors, I felt unable to find the courage to do the right thing by them and repair the damage. I couldn't find the words or the actions to show how badly I felt and how sorry I was. But they rose above this and taught me about tolerance.

They didn't write me off. They didn't dismiss me. They, to this day, have been able to look at me and see a brother instead of a bully. Returning smiles for all my anger. They let me be myself, even if that self spent years being ugly to them. It's a source of strength for me now. That all is not lost. A mistake is a mistake. You, and I, can go on and be who we should be if someone sticks by you. If your family sticks by you. If your community sticks by you. If they can tolerate your weaknesses so they can benefit from your strengths, we all can enjoy a little more excellence. This is, without a doubt, the greatest of all the lessons I have ever learned.

I can't thank them enough.

DEATH WISH

Leftmost in the cover photo is Steve. This seems appropriate because Steve always seemed, er — well, a little bit left-most. It is no accident that everyone else is looking in one direction and Steve another. He always seemed to be a little bit different. He looked at things in a unique way, but his approach was more convoluted than original. And not just from us, but from just about everyone else, too. This was an aspect of Steve that I always found frustrating. But I can credit him with being the single greatest source of my lessons in how important and powerful Tolerance was to achieving excellence.

Steve is an unbelievable mixture of contradictions. He has been a loyal friend of mine since we were 7 years old yet he politicked vigorously, and unsuccessfully, to block me from joining the extended crew when we were fifteen. He possessed less than average intelligence but read a lot and worked hard on his vocabulary and to improve his mental capabilities. He was physically well built and strong but so uncoordinated that he couldn't win a fight with a Girl Scout. He's actually the only person I know whose glasses were broken by a pitched softball that hit him square in the face after he had swung and missed it. But, to do that, Steve had to be at bat. He had to be in the game, and that was Steve's strength. He was involved. Making his contributions. Steve found ways to be part of everything we did, even when his abilities didn't measure up. He could be counted on to be there and pitching in even though we all knew, including him, that the end result usually backfired.

Steve's most memorable talent was for somehow surviving dangerous events, earning him the unwelcome nickname of Death Wish.

A lot of this was his own making, like him losing a fight to a guy who was sitting next to his girlfriend and just watched Steve try to pick her up. Also some of this came at Steve because he just didn't realize what he was doing. Like when he lost a fight to someone he just jokingly gave the finger to, you might call it flipping the bird, who Steve had thought was a friend.

Frightful things beyond his control also followed Steve. Like falling, unhurt, from a moving truck; or rolling his VW Beetle at 60 mph on the grass shoulder of the Southern State Parkway, walking away soaked in gasoline, and then lighting a cigarette to calm his nerves; or getting pushed in front of an oncoming subway train. He survived this episode because he lay down in between the tracks and let the train roll over him, thereby following explicit instructions from a bystander. How he survived the others, we can only guess.

My best moment with Steve came in a pizza place after we had finished that night's six-pack. We were enjoying a snack at our regular place when in walked a drunk, middle aged, CPA looking bald man, with glasses and a perfect pear shaped body, who mistakenly thought I was laughing at him. He attacked, rushed over and grabbed me by the back of the neck.

Steve, who was sitting between me and the drunken CPA, instantly leapt to my defense, "You can't do that to my friend!" He gallantly cried.

While Steve starting wrestling with the Drunken CPA Assassin, dragging the three of us into an innocent floor plant, the rest of us starting roaring with laughter. Real down deep, sidesplitting laughter. We had all come to the same conclusion at the same second - that now we were going to have to save Steve from losing a fight to a drunken, out-of-shape, bald, myopic, forty-something CPA. Our reaction caught the combatants completely off guard and stopped the two of them dead in their tracks. To end the incident, the owner then ejected the CPA and let us off with a warning. But Steve did cover my back, something I would have missed if I had let my frustrations with Steve affect our friendship.

I never tried to change Steve. None of us did. His unique approach to life was what made Steve,...well Steve. Nobody else I have ever met looked at things the way he did, and for all the frustration this caused, it was still the reason we called him our friend.

S K I   T R I P

Near the end of my rookie season with Mahoney's football
team, one of our teammates arranged for us to travel to the
Poconos to play a game against his friends there. Roddy had
moved to Tannersville PA from Flatbush with his father. He still
would come down on weekends to play football with us. He of
course told his friends there about Mahoney's, our team, and
our parties. They told Roddy that it would be great for us to
go there to play them. They claimed that they could beat us in
a game of our rules, 8 on 8, four eligible receivers, two-hand
touch, rushing and blocking. But we had to play on grass. Our
league played on asphalt in a city park.

Having just finished our season in typical fashion, maybe 2 wins
out of 12 games, but never blown out, we got real excited about
a road trip to a ski resort to play a pick-up game against some
new friends of a teammate. This was going to be a great party.

Now, if you were like most people planning a trip, your first
concerns would be trivial stuff like food, shelter and clothing.
Perhaps even transportation and what roads we had to take to

get there. Oh, how mistaken you would be. The first problem to be solved was proof.

At this time the legal drinking age in New York State was 18, my precise age. The legal age in Pennsylvania was 21. A problem. Not just for me, but also for about a third of the team. All of us then needed some acceptable form of ID to present to a bartender to prove we were 21. Proof.

Now we at Mahoney's could be counted on for a sizeable amount of mischief, but we were not big on breaking the law. Buying and selling false ID, as we all know, is a crime. Borrowing or editing ID was close, but it really was only criminal if you had to show it to the police, and we only intended to use it at bars. So, all we had to do was stay out of fights and there would be no chance of having to show the card to a police officer.

There were two preferred forms of ID then, a driver's license or a draft card. The draft card was preferable for borrowing because a license loan would leave your benefactor stranded. Also, there was a physical description on a draft card but no picture. Just find someone with the same height, weight and eye color and you were set. Also, in the post-Viet Nam world of 1975, not having burnt yours still meant something.

I borrowed a draft card from a friend named Jimmy. We were about the same height, he might have been a little heavier than me but there was something else that potentially presented a problem for me. Jimmy was Italian. This is not a bad thing for a person to be; only I wasn't. And besides, Jimmy looked Italian. Very Italian. I looked Irish. Very Irish. The brown hair was okay, but his eyes were brown. Mine, blue. BLUE. Very blue. Or, as it appeared on the Draft Card, he BR; me BL. In the smoky dinge of a mountain bar I didn't think it would matter much. What should have mattered, but never occurred to me, was that he was 22 and I was 18, and looked 16, yet I took the card enthusiastically. Ignorance is bliss.

While I was hectically engaged in securing my proof, there actually were some people who, thankfully, paid attention to the more mundane issues that needed to be organized. Such as:

Field – local high school, on a Sunday morning. No problem.

Room – I have no idea who booked this, but all 25 of us got rooms in the same motel. Punchy was the best at this kind of thing, so we'll give him credit.

Ride – Easy enough. I'd ride with my brother Tommy in his spacious 1955 Olds 88. (Great car. Big, roomy, fast, good radio and the best heater in the world. We were headed for the mountains in January, remember.)

The game was scheduled for Sunday morning. Our convoy of about a dozen cars left Brooklyn about 8:30AM on Saturday for the trip west which lasted until about 2:00 PM. We needed 45 minutes or so to check into the motel and then headed to the bar to meet our adversaries. This was a real good party. You could understand how Roddy would fall in with these guys, they were all right.

Around 5:30, my brother's friend John started to solicit comrades to join him on an little night skiing excursion to Camelback Resort, about 20 minutes away. I was all fired up and ready to do just about anything. Besides, it seemed to me that it was just common sense, in a ski resort, go skiing, kind of like that Rome thing. Apparently, I was the only one using common sense because everyone else told John no. Most were actually laughing about how stupid an idea it was. I think if they were less emphatic about how dumb it really was, I probably would have bailed out. But they only succeeded in ratcheting up my stubborn "I am different" attitude to Warp Factor 5. So, I went.

After the short drive, John and I hustled to the lodge. The lift ticket and equipment rental went for about $30. Plus another $20 was needed as a rental deposit. This was most of my budget for the trip, but it was too late to care now.

I found out that the first thing to be worked out for a rookie skier was getting a good pair of boots. It didn't take long for our resident equipment expert to come up with a pair that he thought would work out well for me. Actually, the boots felt great. I didn't realize it then, but this was actually a bad sign. I should have listened to the danger signals right then. But I didn't. I was fooled. Fooled by the fact that the boots were manufactured by the same company that made my ice skates. A fact I was very ready to share with the equipment rental guy. I was very happy to report that they did indeed feel exactly like my skates.

Next there occurred some discussion by John and the rental guy about how long my skis should be. I think they settled on 3 feet. Didn't matter to me, the boots felt great.

Once we got outside, John told me the beginner's slope was to the right, the moderate to the left and the expert straight ahead. He recommended the beginner's slope, just as a start. I remember it being a long snow bank, no more than 20 feet high. It reminded me of a snow pile in a parking lot after a blizzard of snow had been plowed aside. I thought to myself, "I'm not going to embarrass myself on that! I'm going to start on the moderate slope."

Bad sign number two. The stupidity of this should have been banging me right between the eyes, telling me I'm headed for danger. But, I've been known to take a good bang in the head and not feel it. Besides, the boots felt great.

Now, some of you, especially those with some skiing experience may have noticed I received no instruction from John or the rental guy or anybody about things like stopping, or turning, or bindings. They were relying on me starting on the beginner's slope where there were instructors to do some tutoring. Besides, I felt there was no need to waste time on trivial stuff like knowing what I was doing. I had seen those downhill and slalom guys on TV turning and stopping on a dime. They looked like they were using edges just like ice-skating. I figured it would be just like skating. Besides, the boots felt great.

At, Camelback, the moderate slope went down from the lodge and you took a chairlift back up. My first peek over the edge showed me there were dozens of happy skiers, all smiley as they cruised back and force down the slope. The way they looked made skiing seem easy enough. I told myself "Just take it slow at first." So over I went without another thought.

I felt pretty good, nothing fantastic, no big emotional rush or anything, just good. I had no problem keeping my balance. I was sliding forward nicely sensing a growing breeze on my face. I realized then that I was really starting to gain some speed. It became apparent that there was one small difference in what I was doing and what everyone else was doing. They were all looping and turning and snaking themselves along the slope, smiling. Their smiles quickly turned to surprise and then disgust as they saw me pass by, upright, going straight down the hill increasing in speed and becoming a safety concern for everyone.

"Now collect yourself. You can handle this." I told myself. If I were ice skating, I would slow down by focusing my weight on the ball of one foot and dig an edge in. That didn't work. I was going too fast to shift my weight like that. "Hey, maybe the poles. If I dig them in, I could slow myself down." That was a stupid idea. I had to struggle to maintain my balance as I pulled the poles out of the snow to keep from dropping them.

"Hey, how about not slowing down. The land has to flatten soon, right? You can coast to a stop." One look at the tree line across the bottom shot down that idea. My maiden voyage as a skier made it obvious that speed and stupidity have a logarithmic inverse relationship. For every 5 mph I gained, I lost 25 IQ points.

The call then went out. "Sound the alarms, call out the militia! An idiot was on the mountain, let all beware."

This was getting serious. I had to do something. I was really starting to cook now and the other skiers were getting very pissed that I was creating such a hazard. I had to do something and fast. So I fell. Off to the left. I bounced once, rolled a little bit, eventually coming to a stop all covered in snow, but without any damage. At least I didn't feel any damage. When I looked myself over, I saw both my skis sticking out in funny directions. Did I break my legs? You read about that. It could sometimes take a few seconds to feel the pain from a serious injury. But no, I was fine. Only, my bindings had popped open. A small price to pay to make the world safe from the Horrible Skiing Idiot from Flatbush.

I realized that the bindings' design was pretty cool. A spring wound around my ankle so the skis didn't slide off down the mountain on their own. All I had to do was align my toe in the bracket, step down on the heel clip and they popped back into place.

Now, I was intact, partway down a mountainside with only one way left to go: down. My situation presented itself with a very obvious solution. Ask someone how to get the rest off the way down only S-L-O-W-L-Y. But since I had been ignoring all the bad signs up to this point, I wasn't about to abandon my idiot's thought process now.

The Skiing Idiot returned. He got to his feet. Re-popped his bindings. Adjusted his clothing, took a deep breath and proceeded with his pre-flight checklist. Gloves on, poles at the ready, a couple of knee bends and he pushed off. The boots still felt great. Again, the Skiing Idiot headed straight down the hill. He had made up his mind that the best thing for everybody was for him to get to off that mountain as fast as possible. So his plan went like this, get to the bottom with as few falls as necessary, then on to the chair lift for the ride to the lodge, return the equipment and on to a more comfortable and familiar existence. He would go to the bar.

This turned out to be a three-fall hill, the last fall coming a little too close to the trees for comfort, but I was finally down at the bottom. As I lay in the snow I thanked God that I was safe, that I hadn't hurt anyone else and that I still had my idiot's plan to follow. And damn, my boots still felt great.

Having climbed back to my feet, I aligned my skis and cleaned the binding on my left ski and quickly re-popped the foot's binding back in place. Next, I repeated the process for the right foot. Align ski, clean binding, toe set and step down on my heel and click. But, there was no click. It didn't re-pop. I stomped, jumped, cursed; I even hit it with the pole. Nothing. My heel just sat there, two inches above the ski resting on the suddenly stubborn heel clip.

I started to get desperate. I kicked the trees. I jumped some more. I cursed some more, I even cursed a little more than that. I was putting on a pretty good show for the other skiers who were passing me on the shush line to the chairlift, now very happy to see me off the slopes.

"John could probably help. I've got to find John". But he was nowhere to be found.

After about 30 minutes, or 4 laps, if we're counting how many times each skier passed me to get to the chairlift, it finally clicked.

"WHEW. Thank God" I said aloud.

I got on the end of the shush line. Thinking back, I now realize it must have been a skier who thought of having bank lines snake back and forth to feed customers one-at-a-time to the next available teller. This line started straight down the back and ran to the far end of the shushing area, then turned right for a bit,

U-turned back and forth until you got to the loading zone for the chair. The whole course outlined by strings about rib high.

About halfway along the back straight I noticed that the path was closely bordered on the left by a big tree, its roots creating undulations in the snow for about six feet. As I was acknowledging some congratulations and sympathies from some other shushers (They are skiers when on the slope and shushers when on line), my left ski got caught in a tree root undulation, slipped out to the left and BOING, the binding popped open. (For future reference, anytime something like this happens, please assume cursing occurred, because it did).

The line stopped. The sympathizers on line were touched. The congratulators were disappointed I had let them down. I slunk under the rope, got to the other side of the tree, and went about the business of kicking, cursing, jumping, etc. to re-pop my bindings. At one point I lifted the ski to vertical position and kicked the tree, the offending tree, as hard as I could. Even if the binding didn't re-pop, it would feel good kicking this foul tree. I missed. And fell right on my keister, resulting in the other binding popping open (assume).

"You know, I bet John could help, where was John". But he was nowhere to be found.

After about 45 minutes, or 8 more shush laps, I succeeded in getting the bindings back together. I started toward the back of the line but then a wonderful thing happened. Someone lifted the rope and offered me the spot in front of him. Everyone else on line smiled and nodded their approval of this compassionate gesture. So I started to duck under the rope until someone three positions in front of him stopped me.

"Hey, not there. Get on this side of the roots". He also was lifting the rope for me.

More smiling and nodding. It seems the congratulators had turned to sympathizers sometime during the 8 or so laps that my chore took to complete. I gratefully accepted.

At last, I was re-enshushing. I was very careful navigating that first right turn and started gaining confidence as each successive turn was handled successfully. As you might expect, I began to lose some caution and picked up my pace. Just when it appeared the worst was over, BOING, my right binding popped open again (assume). As I had made the left turn across from the root undulations of the kicking tree, my ski veered right and ... you know the rest.

"You know, I bet John..." you know the rest.

It was about now that I forgot that the boots felt good.

The good news was that by now everyone was a sympathizer, so I hadn't let anyone down. The line stopped, the rope was lifted. The Skiing Idiot went back to his ritual wrestling match with the demonic bindings. Another 25 minutes or so and I was cordially re-admitted as a shusher. Again at the point of my last casualty. I sighed. The line sighed. John was still nowhere to be found.

Say what you want about skiers, but I think they are a kind and compassionate people. They'd have trouble on a NYC subway, but as a rule they're real good people. All except one. The guy right in front of me. Now, I figured one of three things happened to produce this exception to the compassionate skier rule for the skier in front of me. He was either on his first lap by, or he was a congratulator who hadn't' forgiven me, or he was just nasty. Regardless of what the explanation was, he did not approve of me.

I continued to follow my grumpy guide around the rest of the shush path until we finally reached the chair loading zone. I was second. This meant that me and 'Miss Congeniality' would have to share a chair for the ride back to the lodge. Who cares. Life was good again. A short ride up, off the chair, remove the offensive skis, walk - NOT SHUSH – back to the rental guy, retrieve my deposit and shoes, and go to the bar.

I had instinctively returned to my idiot's plan. I assumed I was home free. Just shush into position, hop onto the chair and up we go. This plan went fine until in the act of hopping on to the chair my left binding popped open (assume). Wait a minute. Disassume. I was home free. I'm on the chair. Who cares about the (assume)ing binding.

As I explained this to Grumpy (I had to talk to somebody, 7 second rule, remember?) his facial expression changed from grumpy to something you would only see in the climatic scene of a Hitchcock movie (wait, don't they call his work films? Never mind.) Now why would he get so worked up over this? Didn't he know I had been down there for almost two hours wrestling with these bindings? But then the light blinked on.

"Oh, I have to get off the chair, don't I"? Asked the Skiing Idiot.

"Yeah, asshole, that would be a good idea". Grumpy replied.

I accepted this from him without a word because I was calling myself something a lot worse than asshole. (Assume a lot worse than Skiing Idiot, too.)

"You know, I'll bet John… Hey, I still hadn't seen John. I've got to find John." I said to the Grumpy. He just threw up his arms as I turned to look down at the slope beneath my feet to find John.

"Hey John. Up here."

"Hey Richie. What the (assume) happened to the ski."

"Forget that. I'm done skiing. I'll meet you at the bar. How long you gonna be?"

"Maybe another hour."

"Okay, see you later." To Grumpy, "That was John." Using my best 'told you so face'. In reaction to the mythic John being immediately below us at that very second, the grump now had regressed to the point of just holding his head in his hands and mumbling.

But my success at finding John had not changed the fact that I still had to get off the chair. The Skiing Idiot decided that he needed a new plan.

My ski was dangling under my foot, held to my ankle by the spring. It was swinging pendulum-like at a very definite rhythm. I looked up at the chairlift in front of me. The chairs leveled off for a short straight space, then swung to the right to start the return trip down for more shushers. I was sitting on the left of the chair. Ski swinging, boot, landing area, chairs swing to the right. Swinging left ski. Clear space off to the left of the chairlift.

I got an idea. It was obvious to me that all I had to do was to hop off the chair just as the left ski started a backward beat, plant my right ski, then slap the left ski under my foot, push off to the left with my right foot and dive for cover.

Now, I know that I prefaced this book with a disclaimer that if I represented something in this book that was not quite factual, that it was due to my grey haired enwrapped memory and the lesson I ascribed to the event. But not here. This is as clear as if I wrote this while sitting in the snow immediately afterward. Experienced skiers, when hearing this story, have asked me questions like "How long were you in the hospital?" or "Can I touch the metal plate in the back of your head?" The truth is that this plan worked. Exactly as I had envisioned it. Idiot or not, my plan was going smoothly. Oh, by the way, when I sat up to remove my skis, I found Grumpy just standing there, in shock I think.

"You should be dead, you know." He said.

"Why?" I asked.

He didn't try to explain. He just shushed off to some private corner with his head twitching while sucking his thumb and mumbling to himself. I think this episode may have unnerved him a bit.

I, on the other hand, was feeling ecstatic. Indeed, I had had enough of skiing, (assuming) bindings, shushing and everything else. But now I could dispense with all that and settle myself into the more comfortable setting at the bar. So, I took off the skies and trudged back to the rental guy.

"How was it?" he asked.

"The boots felt great but the damn bindings kept popping open and I couldn't get them back together." I replied.

"Were you stuck down at the chairlift for the intermediate slope."

"Yeah. I went down once and it took me 2 hours to get back up."

"Can I reoutfit you?"

"No, I've had enough."

"Sorry. Here's your deposit and a refund for the rental fee. I can't refund the lift ticket but I owe you. These bindings should have been out of service. That's my fault. I hope you'll come back soon and give us another chance."

This was how you do business. Promise something and then deliver. But if you fail, refund the fee and ask for another chance. It's the right thing. It's justice. You can't do it any better or more 'Flatbush'. I never did ski again, but if I do, I'd have no qualms about going to Camelback, even now over 25 years later.

Now, on to the bar. I was not so flustered with this skiing debacle not to anticipate a nice cold beer. I thanked the rental guy and then asked for directions to the bar. "Go out the door, turn right and go up the ramp. The entrance is on your right."

I got to the door of the bar and went in. I couldn't see a thing for a couple of seconds. Even though it was about 8:00 PM the skiing area was brightly lit by spotlights. So my eyes needed time to adjust to the darkness in the bar.

The first thing I could make out was the silhouette of a large male figure, the bouncer, talking to three female figures.

"I need your ID, please." Said the male voice.

I handed him Jimmy's draft card. He turned to try and angle some of the light fighting its way through window onto the card. He had a badge on. Holy (assume), I just gave my fake proof to cop. Not just a cop, a friggan state trooper. What kind of state is this? Cops for bouncers. I had visions of 'assume the position', strip search, handcuffs, bail hearing, my father's face, flashing through my mind at 60 mph.

"What color are your eyes?"

Nailed! "Brown" I said.

"How much you weigh?"

"Now, about 155, I think that says 170."

"Okay go ahead."

I received the card back and avoided looking into his eyes by focusing on my wallet as I replaced the draft card while walking away. I don't think it would have mattered where my eyes were looking because he was paying far more attention to the girls instead of me. It's possible he couldn't even read the information in that light but was just testing for how I answered. Be that as it may, that was the last time I ever gave anyone false ID.

But I came away with a greater appreciation for how those skiers had treated me despite my ignorance of what I was doing. Their tolerance for my idiotic, and dangerous, behavior on the slope showed me that we might need to wait for the best our neighbors can offer. That it sometimes takes time for a person to find their right path. That we owe it to all members, and ourselves, to stand by those who need more time to learn and experience the world before finding their true paths to excellence.

B O N E Y ' S

The purpose of this book is to describe how my community, my neighborhood, was able to pass along the lessons of life to its members. Members from all walks of life, different careers, different heritages, different strengths and different weaknesses. But all equally welcome.

There was one exception to this welcome. A difference in some people that always seemed to make them excluded in our efforts for excellence and I've always had trouble understanding why. The negative attitude for other races that pervades humanity. I could never fathom how anyone could develop a dislike or hatred for someone else without first finding a reason for his or her feelings. How could anyone hate without basis, without reason.

What we call prejudice.

The next stories look at three events from the library of situations arising from the mixing of the races in Flatbush Brooklyn during the early Seventies. A time when the neighborhood was changing from primarily Irish/Italian working class to primarily black working class, most of who were of Caribbean heritage.

I don't expect to answer any questions or solve race relation problems. But I look at these three stories, which occurred almost simultaneously, involving some of the same people; yet describing behaviors so different that they defy my being able to rationalize the differences.

The first event involved a park that was more than a park. It was a memorial to one of the neighborhood's great people, Mr. Anthony Chiarantano.

Mr. C worked for the phone company. He was a dedicated family man and an active community member. Someone to be celebrated and emulated. The park commemorated how he lived and how he died.

He died trying to help a woman who was being attacked. Whether he knew it or not, the attacker had a knife, and he used it to stab Mr. C to death. Mr. C wasn't the type of person who could turn his back on someone in trouble. He grew up with the code, lived by the code, and became a martyr for the code.

The very fitting memorial to him was a park that contained a beautifully manicured baseball field and a roller hockey rink. Mr. C was a big supporter of the Little League to which he gave his time, energy and expertise.

But the hockey rink was the special accolade here. The part of the memorial that added an extra acknowledgement for this wonderful man.

When his oldest son Danny and his friends started playing hockey on the street, Mr. C realized that something should be done to improve the places that they played. His efforts resulted in the football field at the park on Albany and Farragut getting a partial repavement so there was a smooth surface for them to skate on. Off the street and out of the traffic.

Safety wasn't the only motive, though. The kids needed a better facility because Mr. and Mrs. C, along with Mr. and Mrs. McNeill, got their sons and their friends organized into a team. The Blues. Later he started a second team for their younger brothers, the Canucks, some of who successfully navigated the rites of passage and eventually graduated to the Blues.

The Blues became quite a bit more than a roller hockey team. In typical Flatbush fashion, those of us who played for the Blues ascribe ourselves a community status. A brotherhood. I wasn't part of that original team, but I feel the same pride about having played for this team, the same gratitude to Mr. C and Mr. McNeill for getting it started, as my friends who were original members.

At the beginning, Mr. C. knew as much about hockey as he did about the reproduction habits of mollusk life forms in the shallows around the Hawaiian Islands. But the kids, his kids, the neighborhood kids, liked hockey and he wanted to help them enjoy it. And he got a lot accomplished to make us into a team, a brotherhood and a community.

So, in the memory of this wonderful man, a masterfully constructed hockey rink was included as the centerpiece of Chiarantano Park on 45th Street between Farragut and Glenwood Roads. It became the home ice for the Blues and the Canucks and any other neighborhood kid that wanted to skate and enjoy the greatest sport on earth. (Subjective opinion).

But the park was also there to remind those kids about a great man. A man who taught us that great good can come from living by the code. Great good comes from helping others. From getting involved. From working toward a goal. From doing the right thing.

And then they burned it down.

The way I heard it, that as the neighborhood changed to a primarily black community, one that didn't know Mr. C, that didn't like hockey, that didn't know the code. The kids of that community felt that this hockey court was not a memorial but an eyesore, an insult. A statement that said that though 'WE', the blacks might live here now, 'THEY', the whites, were still here. Still commemorating. Still waving hockey sticks under their noses. At least this is what I was told the kids who did the burning said when they were caught.

"No more of this hockey spit, we want basketball courts."

So they burned it down.

And the city built basketball courts.

————————————

The second event was actually a series of events. Events that occurred rarely but rate on a similar scale as the burning of Chiarantano Park.

One of my teammates on Mahoney's football team drove an orange car. It stood out wherever it went. One of the advantages of an orange car is that you can find it a lot faster when it's parked in a large parking lot. But this loud coloring could also have its shortcomings.

Like if you decided that for fun you would drive the car down Foster Avenue through the Vandeveer Apartments and use the passenger car door to bump black people crossing the street in the buttocks. Not hard enough to hurt them physically, but enough to degrade, humiliate, and infuriate.

Foster Avenue was a convenient route to go from Mahoney's to Brennan's on Nostrand and Avenue D. By taking this way you were able to get a better parking spot on E 29th St closer to Ave D and closer to Brennan's. You also avoided the difficulty that

Nostrand Av presented because it was a one way street when you were circling the nearby streets to find parking.

So Foster Avenue was a road we drove on pretty frequently, especially during football season. I was uncomfortable about all this because the targeting criteria focused on the largeness of the butt of the intended victim. I was uncomfortable about all this because they didn't exclude older people, or feeble people, or young people. I was uncomfortable about all this because this was wrong, it was intolerant, and unjustified. When you acted like an asshole you had to expect to be treated like an asshole. Also, if payback were forthcoming, having an orange car, the only one in the neighborhood, would make it easier for you to be found.

Luckily, we weren't found. I can't lose the thought that if we were found, I would have been caught in a serious philosophical dilemma. Cover my friends' backs or rise up to secure justice in my community. I settled on a middle road. I told the close friend who was the owner of the orange car that I couldn't ride along if he was going to go 'Butt Hunting' on Foster Avenue. He told me not to worry that he realized it was a pretty stupid thing to do and was going to stop anyway.

But I still felt, and feel today, that there has to be a better way. We can't succeed if we constantly exclude the contributions of a whole segment of our community because of some inconsequential thing like color of skin, or religious belief, or career choice, or anything else that ignores an individual's talents and drowns them under a prejudice against a group.

The two proceeding stories seem to indicate that things might be hopeless for the peaceful coexistence of the races in Flatbush.

But then came Boney's.

Boney's was a bar in the transition zone between the changing communities where it was hard to distinguish whether you were in a black neighborhood or white. Church and Foster Avenues being the approximate North-South borders and Utica and Flatbush Avenues being the East-West.

This story occurs on a nice Autumn Sunday afternoon. We had enjoyed our normal bar league football game at the park and now had a taste for a party with a little different flavor. Phil's brother Tommy and cousin Pat knew just the place.

There were about 20 patrons in the bar when we arrived. All black. A few couples in the booths and the rest at the bar. A quiet atmosphere with little going on but drinks and soft conversation.

Then, in walked about twenty white guys in Mahoney's Bar and Grill football shirts. The patrons and bartender became very concerned, some probably even scared. Though total numbers were pretty even, they had about 5 or 6 women there. Their idea of a quiet Sunday drink or two seemed to be in trouble. I can't say we were welcomed with open arms.

"How much for a pitcher of Bud?" was the question that broke the silence.

"Five dollars."

"Five dollars each." Was Pat's way of announcing the bar pool was open. Tommy followed with his call "Dollar for the jukebox."

"Could we have two pitchers and some glasses please?"

"Excuse me," interrupted Tommy, wearing his huge smile, "Can I have change for the juke box first?"

"Yeah, sure. Here you go. 12 quarters. And for you, two pitchers of beer. That'll be ten dollars."

The football players interrupted their own conversations to pass their dues forward towards the bar. Just then the music kicked in, the opening phrases of 'Pick Up the Pieces' by the Average White Band. A great funky jazz song. A great dancing song. Some of the football players commenced with pouring beers and passing them around. Some were still scanning the selection on the jukebox. Some started what in generous circles might be called dancing.

"Excuse me, but would it be a problem if we put the Giants game on TV?"

"Sure, why not."

As the bartender went to the back to turn on the TV, no remotes then, he had to stand on a chair, he gave a shrug to the 3 booths that lined the back wall. Once he succeeded in getting the game on, he was interrupted with one more request.

"Excuse me, do you know how to make Alabama Slammers?"

"No, let's get some Kamikazes."

"No I'd rather have Slammers."

"Hey, we'll get both. That is if you know how to make them?" Attention turned from the two Mahoney's players to the bartender.

"No idea. Alabama what?"

A devilish grin crossed the face of the man in control of the pot, Pat, "Wanna learn?"

Devilish grin returned, "Are they good?"

"If its okay by you, I'll make a batch and you can see for yourself?"

To facilitate self-service, we normally would get our Kamikazes and Slammers in small water pitchers used for whiskey drinkers, but Boney didn't have any. So we had to settle for empty orange juice bottles. Once mixed, Boney was served the first shot out of the Kamikaze container.

His face lit up. "That spit's good!"

He was equally enamored of the Alabama Slammers.

"Shots up!" went the call.

Dozens of shot glasses began to appear on the bar and instantly being filled with one or the other drinks and passed out to all in attendance who wanted one, black and white alike. I turned to the man sitting alone at the end of the bar by the window. He seemed to be oblivious to everything that was going on around him.

"You want one?"

"What?"

"Do you want to try one of these shots?" I asked again, holding a Kamikaze and Slammer out in front of me for him to choose.

Boney walked up, "These are good spit, Turner. Try one."

Turner elected the Kamikaze and we drank them down. He smiled broadly, gave me a pat me on the back and said "Thanks."

I turned and saw some of my teammates doing the same thing to the people at the tables and the others at the bar. Anyone who wanted had their choice of shots.

Before we left about five hours later, dancing was shared with the women, jokes were told and football games were enjoyed. There was music, drinks and camaraderie. This community of 20 black and 20 whites, each putting aside fear and prejudice for one afternoon had a great time together.

For about five hours, Boney's had become the one spot in the world that showed that communities are not geographic locations. They are shared experiences, shared enjoyments and shared feelings.

In Flatbush, there was a black community that burned down hockey rinks, a white community that went around smashing car doors into pedestrians' backsides and a Boney's community that put all that aside and welcomed any who could gather with tolerance for differences and find something in common for all to enjoy.

I liked the Boney's community best.

Even though it illustrates to me that the code could cross racial lines and unite black and white, it added to the regret that it eventually would not. The inability of the members of each community to adopt a Boney's community would disperse the members to two different and lesser worlds.

But Boney's showed us that it doesn't have to and gave us something to work for in the future.

PART V - CELEBRATION

Then comes the party.

How better to show that we're all in this together. Your problems are my problems. Your successes are shared by all. The rewards that come from that success will take place. Be you. I like you. Smile about being you. We're all smiling because you're here. And smiling even brighter because you brought someone new with you. Your friend is my friend. Give me a dollar for the jukebox.

What a community puts into its celebrations it gets back in excellence. The better able we are at spending a good time together the easier it will seem to cover each other's backs, the easier to go out and find our own road, the easier to work for everyone's just rewards, the easier to allow everyone their own viewpoint. The celebration is the mortar that holds these building blocks of excellence together.

It is at celebrations that we proclaim our kinship. The singing, the dancing, the laughing all supply the connection needed to provide the substance to congratulatory pats on the back or compassionate expressions of sympathy. We show we care at celebrations by sharing the emotions of life with our neighbors, friends and family.

It is also at celebrations that we officially acknowledge new membership. Whether those acknowledgements are formal, as at weddings and christenings, or informal as when someone brings a few friends from work to meet the guys from the old neighborhood.

I think it is our attitude toward celebrations that separates those of us from Flatbush from others. What ingredients are needed to make a few beers at a bar become a full-fledged community cementing celebration.

PICNICS AND WEDDINGS

Occasions to celebrate are cherished in my family. A tradition of having a large family picnic grew out of an attempt to celebrate my grandmother's birthday. Sadie was recognized as the matriarch of my mother's family, which included Sadie's brothers' and sisters' families as well. In fact one of those sisters shared Aug. 11 with Sadie as a birthday. The typical attendance for these picnics was somewhere close to 100 people. Food, drink, softball, more food, another drink and a lot of fun and jokes were shared. But, the highlight of every picnic was the singing. My Uncle Jimmy's George M. Cohan medley offering some sublime fun. My father's raucous rendition of "Phil, the Fluter's Ball' was a bit more to the ridiculous side of the equation. Various aunts, uncles, siblings and cousins also chipping in to the sing-alongs. Equally important was the non-participation of those few family members (especially me) who must have been in the bathroom when God was handing out the musical DNA. I'm proud to report, and you'd agree if you heard him, that my brother Bobby must have been the happy recipient of all that extra musical talent that had bypassed us of limited capacity. His rendition of "O Danny Boy" usually ended the singing, but for one song. We always closed the picnic with a hands-holding chorus of 'There's a New World Somewhere'. Our anthem of togetherness.

Our picnic antics were carried over to our weddings, where they took on a whole new character.

My sister Madelyn, cousin Eileen and brother Tommy all had more generally acceptable wedding receptions. We all had a great time at each, but they were missing a new tradition that sort of grew out of a moment of impatient inspiration at my wedding. The ushers were introduced wearing the bridesmaids' large, colorful, floppy, straw hats.

This happened because my father and I extended the cocktail hour by about 15 extra minutes so we could enjoy a couple of beers with his brother-in-law, and my godfather, Uncle Bert. I hadn't seen him for about ten years and had finally caught up to him just as they were closing up the cocktail hour. The bartender was eager to please when he heard about the reunion. We sat, sipped, and talked merrily not realizing that the 135 or so guests who were staring at our backs as we drank in the loft overlooking the dance floor might have been less than pleased. The bridal party were distracting themselves with a small, impromptu floppy hat fashion show upstairs as they waited. My wife and I decided that there couldn't be a better way to kick off a marriage than to embarrass our ushers by having them introduced like that. They agreed instantly. The audience also approved of this whacky if untraditional idea. Having the emcee introduce my wife and I twice, to entice everyone into mistakenly thinking I would be wearing the veil, only helped with the moment.

From here, the zaniness grew into a family tradition. My cousin Kathy got married a few years later on October 30th, so we all bought Halloween masks to be put on just before the introductions began. The mask highlights went to my father's pitch black, waist length beard, to go with his snow white crop of hair and my follically challenged Uncle Joe's bald, green skinned alien mask that fully covered his head. The next theme was for all of us to wear sunglasses, to commemorate my Uncle Bob's and Aunt Gerry's habit of jamming themselves and all five children, each wearing sunglasses, into their Volkswagen for a drive around the highways waiting for someone to stare at them. In perfect synchronization they would all slowly turn their heads and stare back. We also did hats, some were even illuminated. Next came the wedding of unknown wedding guests, we all wore decorated paper bags on our heads.

My favorite wedding moment came when a woman guest jumped up onstage during the band's first break and loudly announced that it was time for everyone to line up for aerobics. My generation of cousins quickly mustered into about five lines of eager and faithful aerobinauts. At the last moment, two very fit and trim young ladies from the other family fell in next to me in the last tier.

"It might be a good idea for you to wait a minute before joining in." I suggested.

"Oh, we're fine. We've been doing aerobics for over a year now." They reassured me.

"Suit yourself. But don't say I didn't warn you." I absolved myself.

"Okay, everyone. Let's start with a warm-up." Chimed our exercise leader. "Let's start by marching in place, swinging your arms." Full compliance. "Good, now let's get those shoulders loosened. Arms at your sides. Bring them up slowly til they're even with your shoulders. Good, good."

"Now let's get those lower backs stretched out. Everyone on their Knees. Ladies! Ladies, remember your modesty." It was here that the two 'interlopers started looking slightly askance. "Sitting on your heels I want all of you to reach up as high as you can. Great. Now bend forward slowly. Good. Reach back up. Bend forward slowly." An absurd picture, every aerobinaut was dressed to the nines, on their knees, and steadily and repeatedly stretching our arms up to the ceiling and then bending forward until our fingers touched the dance floor in front of us.

"Great. You all look absolutely great! Now repeat after me: We love you Aunt Gerry. We love you Aunt Gerry. We love you Aunt Gerry." Enthusiastic full compliance.

My newly in-lawed neighbors, without losing the rhythm, looked at me and asked together. "Whose Aunt Gerry?"

"She is." I said, pointing at the instructor.

"Ooooh." The two newest, and grinning, members of the family said in unison. They seemed very happy to have joined a family that could offer fun with such originality and style. Then they both turned their head down and continued, along with the rest of us. "We love you Aunt Gerry. We love you Aunt Gerry. We love you Aunt Gerry."

And we certainly do.

B R A C E L E T S

Next to Joey D in our cover picture comes me. Partially obscured but visible enough to see that I'm laughing a little harder than the others. At this time, it was laughter and fun that I wanted more than anything else. Also, as appropriate as Steve being left-most and Joey being hind-most is me being obscured-most. As I mentioned, I kept a lot of what I thought, felt and believed to myself. I lived as I thought others thought I should. Obscured.

I have been trying to clarify the picture you should see there and have approached success with the exercise of writing this book. But I want to put my own issues aside for a bit and concentrate on the others in my life who I watched and from whom I learned.

And when it comes to celebrating, there's no one better to learn from than Joe R. Joe was a natural comedian and our best drinker. He is leaning in, sort of mugging, trying to get some more laughs. Keep the partying going. Joe has a unique talent for partying. No, not just drinking. Not just dancing. Partying for us had to include including. Others with us and us with others. He's especially good at seeking out new places to go and forging new friendships. He's taken me to many places we've never been before, spent a few hours partying and left with a new hangout and new friends.

But Joe and I had something else that was special. A sense and understanding of one another that prevented us from ever getting away with lying to the other. Almost a silent communication. This aspect of our friendship always made me feel that I had someone with me even if for the moment I was alone.

But this could also add some fun.

Joe R and I had just arrived at The Bawdy Barn in the Hamptons to begin a Saturday night of fun and partying. We proceeded to one of our regular spots next to the big, wide post holding up the roof in the middle of the barroom. There were about 6 or 7 of our friends already there.

After getting my beer from our good buddy Chris, different Chris — the bartender, I started to scan the room. Looking towards the dance floor doors just opposite us, my eyes quickly focused on an attractive girl of about 19, who was standing next to three guys and another girl, who was kind of mousy and nerdy looking. The guys, however, were full-fledged, card-carrying dorks. One was even still wearing his rubber pocket protector with 4 pens in it.

In spite of the rare appearance of a team of computer programmers at the Bawdy Barn, the main attraction was the girl in the middle. She wasn't that bad looking. But that's not what drew my attention to her. She was waving her arms around like a Carnival spider ride as she dominated any and all conversation between her and her nerdly audience. To make matters worse, she was wearing about four gold bracelets on each arm, two sets of dangling earrings and about 5 gold chains or necklaces. The bracelets were especially annoying because they made a horrible racket, even from 15 feet away, as she waved her arms as she talked. And it looked like she was never going to shut up.

"I'm not in the mood for this." I said.

"That's been going on for at least a half hour. And it's giving me a headache." Said one of my friends at the bar.

"Joe, we're going to have to do something about this. Go around that way, past the dance floor, I'll go the other way, meet me at that girl, and pick me up." I said. A nod from Joe and we were off without further conversation, preparation, or planning.

He took a little longer to get into position because of the crowd outside the dance floor doors, so I hesitated a few stools down from our intended target until he got in position. Then we pounced.

As I approached, Miss Bracelets was facing in my direction, with her back to Mousy, both on stools, and facing the three rapt dorks who were standing about three steps away. They were mesmerized by her every word, or perhaps hypnotized by her every shiny, clinking movement.

"Excuse me," I interrupted "did you drop something? I thought I saw something fall over there." I was pointing under her left elbow, between the stools and the bar.

Joe's timing was perfect. "Yeah, I think I saw something roll over here." As he pointed down behind Mousy.

"MY MOTHER"S RING!!!!" Bracelets screamed. "Oh, you've got to help me find my mother's ring." She pleaded.

The three dorks dove right in. Bracelets was peering down from her stool while Mousy was struggling between helping to look and maintaining her modesty, as the three males were busy crawling about under her stool. Joe stepped to his right. I sidled to my left. And we both left, going in the opposite directions, melting into the crowd. Back to our spots by the pole.

'That should do it." We said as we joined our now laughing friends, being comfortably obscured by that big pole, to resume our beer drinking. About 5 minutes later, Bracelets, who had apparently climbed off her throne to dig in, stuck her head up long enough to ask the bartender for a flashlight.

"Chris. Chris, come here." I tried to get his attention.

"Just a minute, that girl lost a ring or something." He replied.

"No, she didn't." I said. Something in the tone of my voice and in our expressions made him stop his search and come over.

"Okay, whaddya do?" he asked.

When we explained what we did and why, he smiled, shook his head and regretfully informed our nerdly damsel in distress that the flashlight was missing. This upset Bracelets so much she up and left us. Her three admirers and female support in tow.

Okay, I agree, this may not be the best example of tolerance for other people, or of doing the right thing. But, Joe and I had successfully, benignly and creatively improved the prospects of a fine, fun evening. No planning. No rehearsals. Nothing at work but our knowledge of each other and a similar imagination. And a steadfast belief that we will cover each other's back no matter what.

As I mentioned with Phil, sometimes exceptions prove the rule. No, we didn't go out of our way to include Bracelets and company in our community, to our discredit. What this story is about is how Joe and I knew each other well enough that we could relieve our friends from Bracelets annoying behavior without causing any real damage to anyone. We could then proceed with our own celebration.

Which, it turns out got a little bigger and better when the three guys to our left showed their appreciation for our relieving their headache from Bracelets by buying Joe and I a beer. Then the two guys on the right also paid for a round for us. This began a summer long connection to these five other regulars at the Bawdy Barn. We may not have been very welcoming of Bracelets and her crew but we found five new friends for our less than great behavior. So there was a redeeming result to our failure.

Oh, and for the record, Bracelets wasn't wearing any rings.

THE SUMMER
OF '74 — PART I

If I had to pick the moment in my life when I first started to really understand and appreciate the power of community and the energy gleaned from one's family and friends, it most certainly would have been the Summer of 1974.

During 1974 great and wonderful things happened for me. I turned 18 that summer. This meant that I no longer had to struggle with even the smallest amount of guilt about going into a bar being underage. This summer also included the blossoming of my relationship with my future wife, Mary. A summer that contained a number of personal and private milestones four of which I want to share with you: high school graduation, a canoe trip, a trip to the Hamptons and a compliment, all examples of the camaraderie we had in this community and how the celebration of that camaraderie could lead to excellent things. The trip to the Hamptons will be presented in the next chapter but the other three are combined here.

First, the compliment.

As I have said and will repeat, my home bar was Mahoney's, on Ave D and East 42nd Street. It would become the headquarters of one of the great communities of Flatbush. The people who came to Mahoney's, the community I'm referring to, were looking for a place to smile, laugh and be with other people that let them breathe, or talk, or just think, worry free. It was not unusual for close sub-communities to grow from the meeting of people from different parishes, age groups and career choices.

At this time the bar was owned by a man named Jimmy, but it was run by Billy. Since Jimmy was rarely there, Billy was the main reason Mahoney's was run as well as it was. Billy took his responsibilities seriously. Sometimes he was required to tell the customers things they didn't want to hear. This created some resentment from a portion of the patrons. In fact, a lot of these patrons actually told me Billy was not a 'good guy'. Mostly this meant that they felt he should buy back more drinks. Buy backs were a common practice in Flatbush neighborhood bars. Usually a regular customer could expect one out of every four or five beers to be free of charge.

As I said, I turned 18 that summer, at the end of July. Eighteen was legal drinking age in New York then. But there were occasions when I didn't wait until the State recognized that I was old enough to go into a bar. Billy had a unique way of handling my underage presence at Mahoney's. He would quietly walk around the bar, and without a word to me but with a knowing grin, gently remove the glass from my hand and walk back to his bartending responsibilities. No 'excuse me'. No conversations. No ejection. But, still no alcohol.

It was on a Sunday when I finally did turn 18. I showed up at Mahoney's that Friday before to meet my friends for a road trip to Breezy Point and Kennedy's Pier Bar and Grill. As usual, I was the first of us to arrive. I said hello to just about everybody, including Billy, and waited, without a drink, for all of them to show up, so we could leave.

After spending the usual good time with the live music and a few friends who summer at Breezy Point, we decided it was time to head back to Mahoney's. We got back there a little after midnight. As expected, the party was just starting to kick in. Mahoney's was the place to end the night, so prime hours were from 1AM to closing, at 4AM.

I actually saw no point in returning to Mahoney's since Billy knew I was still underage but everyone else said we were going to meet up with some people and pick somewhere else to go. When we arrived, we sidled to our preferred spot under the television by the front window, me standing with my back to the cigarette machine. Everyone I was with got a beer, but I just avoided the subject and stared out the window waiting patiently for him or her to decide on our ultimate destination.

"Happy Birthday!" Said a voice to my right. I turned and there stood Billy with a broad smile and a full glass of beer.

"Thanks." I said, with a little bit of hesitation.

With a nod, Billy turned and went back behind the bar.

For the next three hours, or so, I never had to pay for a drink. Not only did I think of this as an acknowledgement of my birthday but also Billy's idea of a just welcome. He had taken a number of glasses from my hand over the past year, so I think he felt he had a duty to replace them. I didn't think that this was necessary, but I really appreciated the gesture. Money wasn't exactly a common resource for me at this time. This very subtle (I don't think anyone else noticed) compliment made a very solid impression on me. It started a pretty good friendship with a quality guy. A friendship too many others could have gotten into if they could have respected the fact that Billy had a job to do and sometimes that meant he might have to do some things you didn't like. Just a bit more tolerance for another's responsibilities and you reap the rewards of another friendship. I believe there is a common characteristic of those that couldn't tolerate Billy's responsibilities as a bartender. They expected something from you first, and then they could give friendship back. Billy giving more buybacks, or another drink past where it was wise, then they could make friends with him. A me first attitude. Greed.

I always felt that when you did this, you cut yourself off from a lot of what people can give by expecting it up front. Let them bring at their own speed and their own comfort level. That way you know that it comes without pretense or question.

This is also not at all welcoming. Billy made me feel like I was already part of the Mahoney's community with that first ceremonious beer. Sometimes we are welcomed into a community with a whack on our neo-natal backsides. Sometimes it's a seat assignment next to the sideboard in a classroom. Sometimes it's a semi-formal, catered dinner with people wearing tuxedos and bags on their heads and doing aerobics on the dance floor. The only prerequisite for entry is that you show up to be counted. Join in, help out, welcome others and then have fun.

My graduation story is less warming but even more important.

About a month before this event happened, I graduated from Tech. Brooklyn Technical High School, that is. At 9:00 am on the second to last Wednesday of June 1974, the 998 people in my graduating class gathered in the gym at Brooklyn Tech. Yeah, I know, that's a lot of people. No, the ceremony didn't take 5 hours. Only awards were presented at the ceremony, we all had to go back to our homeroom afterwards to pick up our diplomas. The school auditorium only sat about 2,500 people so the seating was limited. Along with the seating constraints, job demands prevented my father from attending.

My mother did go with me. We took the train together to school. It was probably pretty cool for her to go because one of the houses she lived in before moving as a teenager to our house on 37th Street was only two blocks from my school. She sort of got to go home again.

The graduates took up the entire bottom level. Parents and guests sat on floors 2 through 4. My homeroom was on the 6th floor so I told Mom to sit near the door on the 4th floor that was closest for an easier rendezvous later. She could wait in her seat so I could zip upstairs, get my diploma, zip back down to her and then we could zip home. I guess all that zipping gave her, and the rest of my family, the idea that I wasn't expecting a big deal to be made out of my graduation. And I wasn't. Looking back, I regret having done this to my family, especially my father. Part of a relationship is sharing. Sharing the trials and sharing the accomplishments. I prevented them from sharing their congratulations and pride with me and me sharing my sense of accomplishment with them. I excluded them from celebrating this with me and we all suffered for it.

But, my friends and I did make a big deal of it. We had a pretty good party together the night before at Skee's. Chris, Joey D, and I were all graduating that week. Phil had the year before; Joe R would the year after.

The night had some highlights. First was me loudly declaring that the drinks were on me, for the entire bar. That amounted to us and old Mr. Grady. He liked the gesture, but my friends and the bartender didn't think the joke was as funny as I did.

The second highlight came unexpectedly during a commercial break from whatever baseball game we were watching. Most probably the Yankees, not the Mets. Actually, definitely the Yankees. You see the commercial was a Schaefer Beer commercial. While I could be wrong that Schaefer was the Yankees sponsor at this time, I knew that Rheingold was the Met's beer sponsor. My uncle worked for Rheingold, which meant we ere still getting a generous share of Met's and Rheingold souvenirs on a fairly regular basis.

Why is this so important? Because it was the first time we had seen the Schaefer commercial that introduced the 'Ride the River" jingle that celebrated canoeing. We went crazy. Not only did most of us prefer Schaefer, but also we were going canoeing that next weekend. Having the people who brewed our preferred beer give us an anthem for our trip seemed pretty special. We started singing the "Ride the River' song at every lull moment between the shots, jokes, and innings. We thought our singing sounded great until Mr. Grady got up and left. It was almost an hour and a half before his usual departure time. Apparently, our singing made it one of the rare occasions that Mrs. Grady was more pleasant company than the people at Skee's.

But our fun was not to be stopped, only delayed by a couple of days and moved about 110 miles northwest to a town called Narrowsburg on the banks of the Delaware River.

In between a series of events that could have been the funniest of our lives we did manage to climb into the canoes for a couple of hours. The rest of the trip was one comic episode after another made all the more special because of the community of people included on the trip.

We drove up in three cars. Charlie's, with Bobby; Phil's, with Steve and Joey D; and Chris' with Joe R and me. Charlie was a thirty-something, single, and a wealthy banker/lawyer who took a liking to us and a liking to taking us canoeing. He became a good-natured butt of a sizable number of jokes, most from Steve and most in bad taste.

In the days between our graduation party and the canoe trip, Phil saw an interview with Bowie Kuhn, then Commissioner of Baseball. (We pronounce the name Bowie (think dog bark) Kunn.) The result of this was Phil answering any and all questions asked of Mr. Kunn, "Well, I'm sure happy to be here" in his best imitation of a slow Southern drawl. We usually used this to let someone else know they were rambling on stupidly or that the joke attempt had failed. It was best when Phil was the person needing the lesson. This became our running gag for the weekend.

Charlie had reserved a campsite between Rte 97 and the Delaware River about five miles east of the center of Narrowsburg. It was a Boy Scout facility of eight lean-tos paired off and spread west to east across about twelve acres of land. It was populated by tall stately pine trees that let in little sunlight.

Here and there were interspersed clumps of brush and bushes. Having stayed here before, we knew exactly which lean-to we wanted. It was one of the two lying furthest west and in a direct line from the parking lot as you walked across the footbridge toward the largest of the clumps of bushes.

It was dusk when we arrived. To get to our preferred lean-to, we had to cross that small footbridge which spanned a fast running stream perhaps 15 – 20 feet across and maybe two feet deep. The anchor for the bridge was a 50 gallon steel drum filled with concrete and sunk into the middle of the stream. The bridge itself was made of planks about three foot wide and not very strong looking. It was in fact extremely sturdy. Most of us either knew it was actually very safe or were undismayed by its apparent shakiness.

Not so Joey D.

Hugging his backpack close to his chest, Joey sidled across one sliding step at a time, staring down at the swirling, rapid water. We had two people encouraging his every step from each side of the bridge, lighting his way with flashlights in the dimness of the tree covered dusk. It took him about 2 to 3 minutes for a ten second crossing. Perhaps, Joey D's lack of swimming prowess made him a little afraid of the water.

This delay wouldn't have mattered to any of us if we didn't have a lot of essential gear and supplies to carry across the bridge and the 300 yards or so to get to our lean-to. Two big coolers and one small. The food and beer. Since Charlie could be expected at any minute we needed to get the contraband beer over to our camp and quickly stashed. Each of us also had a pack and a sleeping bag, plus Phil had his Wilderness Survival Kit; the lantern his parents used on their honeymoon, a hatchet, and his BB gun. All this had to be carried to our lean-to without Joey D's help because of the footbridge.

For the uninitiated, a lean-to is a three-sided shed with a wooden platform for a floor and facing a brick Bar-B-Que/fireplace that was provided for heat and cooking. The roof extended out over the open space in front to help keep out the weather and to capture the heat and light from the fire.

But we didn't need a fire. It was a toasty warm June evening and we had the honeymoon lantern, powered by Kerosene. Phil lit it right away as the rest of us tried to get settled. We opened a beer each, turned on the radio and staked out the sleeping floor plan. Unfortunately, the lantern turned completely black within about 20 seconds. I guess this was why Phil's parents used it on their honeymoon and never since.

"Well, Bowie (bark) how do feel about the lantern going black?"
"Well, I'm sure glad to be here."

Being deprived of our light source, we then had to resort to plan B and light the fireplace. Search parties were organized and sent out to find wood and kindling. Joe R and I going off westward and Steve and Bobby heading to the brush behind us. Joe and

I were interrupted in our search by news that somebody was in one of our lean-tos. Well, it wasn't really ours. The trespassers had taken one that was intended for some of the kids that the Sergeant Major from Fort Hamilton brought with him. The Sergeant Major was an old Army buddy of Charlie's and they had agreed to meet up at the campsite with some kids from their neighborhoods. This created a small cultural confrontation. In 1974 the Disco era was just beginning, and it was centered in the Bay Ridge and Fort Hamilton sections of Brooklyn. Disco was very unappreciated in Flatbush. In fact, we looked on it as some kind of social malaise and questioned the manliness of anyone who would put on silk flowery shirts, high heels and go prancing around on a dance floor.

Plus, the Fort Hamilton contingent was all rookies at canoe trips. We had been going up here with Charlie for about 3 years with Bobby, Joe R and I as the most frequent attendees. The Fort Hamilton/Bay Ridge kids were there for the first time and really ill prepared for their weekend in the country.

Joe R and I had not gone 50 yards when one of these guys came running up to report the trespassers to the Fort Hamilton/Bay Ridge disco fags (FHBRD fags, for the rest of this story) in our companion lean-to about 25 yards to our left. We joined up with them for the 200-yard run to the far side of the campgrounds to find out what was going on.

When we arrived at the lean-to we saw three men inside the lean-to, already bedded down for the evening in their sleeping bags and not very interested in hearing about rental fees and trespassing. Joe and I could have cared less if they stayed or not. We were set. These guys weren't friends of ours. But, we couldn't understand why the other FHBRD fags weren't being more forceful in trying to evict the trespassers. Doing more to cover their friends' backs. We decided that they needed all our help.

Joe and I hurried back to our lean-to with the news of trespassers in our camp and the inability of the FHBRD fags to handle it. Every one of us leapt to the call to arms. Our compatriots agreed that there was no way that a bunch of Fort Hamilton Bay Ridge Disco fags could handle this without our help. We all started to run to the arena of controversy when we were stopped dead in our tracks by a sickly thud and some quiet groaning. It seems that the eave overhanging the front of our lean-to was the exact same height as the crown of Phil's head.

"I'm okay. I'm okay." He said, as everyone gathered around to check on him.

After finally getting Phil vertical and mobile, we headed off to confront the interlopers at the eastern most lean-to. There were now about 25 FHBRD fags surrounding the lean-to commanding and demanding that these three men leave forthwith.

They were ignored.

Joe and I gravitated to the blond FHBRD fag who had accompanied us before who was quietly laughing at how stupid it was for 25 guys to allow three to ignore them. So he acted.

"Hey, one of them 's gotta gun!" he yelled.

He, Joe R and I ducked behind a nearby tree laughing out loud as we watched the two dozen or so FHBRD fags scatter behind whatever cover they could find doing an excellent imitation of the Keystone Kops. We weren't hiding from the nonexistent gun, just keeping up the ruse and protecting ourselves from the FHBRD fag stampede that followed. It was while we were behind that tree that we promoted our new friend to an honorary citizen of Flatbush.

All the other Flatbush citizens, especially Chris, found this lack of intestinal fortitude disgusting and walked back to our beer, chips and music, albeit in the lanternless and fireless dim of the deepening dusk. We had better things to do than witness such a shameful display of weakness.

It was at this time that Joe R and I were brought up to date on the other problem that had arisen and interrupted Bobby and Steve's search for firewood. The second foraging pair came back reporting harassment from one of the other lean-tos. While Joe and I were checking into trespassing, and forgetting about our firewood responsibilities, they were dealing with FHBRD fags with unacceptable attitudes. Steve and Bobby had been confronted by about seven FHBRD fags who were cursing and insulting them as they searched in the bushes behind their lean-to which was about 100 yards off to our right.

Such inhospitality could not go unavenged. But, in the middle of our planning how to go about exacting our revenge, something far more serious had come up. Bobby came running up to report that Charlie was coming with two State Troopers to take care of the gun-toting trespassers. Knowing Charlie would seek us out first for a report, we all came on the same disturbing thought at once:

"Spit, we gotta hide the beer!"

Everyone jumped to action. Joe R and I grabbed one cooler and quickly moved it into the bushes. Joey D and Bobby had the other one right behind us. Steve came behind holding some open cans.

THUD!!!

Phil was holding his head. Chris was holding Phil.

"I'm okay. I'm okay." Phil and the beam again.

It quickly became apparent that they were approaching faster than we could complete the necessary clean up, so while the others continued to attend to our campsite, Joe R, Bobby and I went out to intercept Charlie and the Troopers and then lead them away from our contraband beer and toward the trespassers.

I'll never forget the view we were confronted with.

The land was slightly uphill for us and downhill for Charlie and the troopers. The two troopers, both carrying shotguns, were striding between the large, grey-trunked pine trees crunching needles and cones under every long deliberate step in the last dregs of light of the rapidly setting sun. They were each about 6'5", built like linebackers, and still wearing their sunglasses; mirrored sunglasses.

We had to stop before reaching them because all three of us were on the verge of busting out in laughter. No, not at the sunglasses, but at Charlie and his strutting along with the two towering Troopers. Charlie reminded me of the little dog in the Bugs Bunny cartoon. The classic one where Bugs is walking through Brooklyn dressed in his best Little Lord Fauntleroy outfit and is waylaid by a band of street dogs led by a huge Bulldog named Spike. Spike had a sidekick, a small terrier that constantly capered and tittered at his side until Spike got fed up with the gnat act and socked the little terrier into a nearby wall.

It looked like that at any minute, one, or both, of the troopers were about to Spike sock Charlie into a nearby tree to stop his capering and tittering.

We succeeded in hiding our amusement at their appearance and then pointed them toward the correct lean-to, falling in behind to witness the show. This procession grew to about 20 more campers, but no one else from Flatbush bothered to make the trip. Almost all of the FHBRD fags were skipping and jostling for position safely behind the two large troopers but still have a good enough view of the trespassers faces when they got a load of this.

It was worth the walk, but only just. The first trespasser was poked on his shoulder by the barrel of a shotgun. His eyes bugged out like he was auditioning for a toon part in 'Roger Rabbit'. The others meekly and quietly got up, got packed and stomped off with Charlie and the troopers. To the great disappointment of the FHBRD fags there was no gun anywhere to be seen.

By the time Bobby, Joe R and I parted company with our new honorary Flatbush citizen and got back to the lean-to, the others had reconvened the party. Music was blaring, beers were slurping and personality traits, such as big lips, being laughed at. We joined right in.

All of us settled down comfortably arrayed into our assigned sleeping positions. Joe R and I sole to sole lying across the front closest to the cold, dark fireplace. The other 5 elbow to elbow across the back. Suddenly, a group of FHBRD fags crossed in front of our lean-to noisily interrupting our peace.

"Hey, that's them." Said Bobby and Steve simultaneously. "The suckers that were giving us grief."

"Plug 'em Bowie" came the unanimous call for justice.

Phil sprung to action. Landing full force on my stomach BB gun at the ready his elbows knocking out all the breath I had.

"Hold still!" commanded Phil.

"I'm trying." I wheezed.

After firing off about 15 rounds into the darkness and in the general direction of the noise, we all told Phil that he should stop. They seemed too far away for the BB gun to reach. He didn't agree but finally succumbed to our armistice proposal.

Reluctantly, Phil went back to his spot. But only for about 15 minutes. When the noise indicated that the 'enemy' was on their return voyage, Gunner Phil again sprung into action. This time on Joe R's stomach.

"Hold still!" commanded Phil.

"I'm trying." Joe wheezed.

Again, after 15 or so rounds, and general agreement that they were out of range, Phil again pulled back to his original position to resume his well-earned R&R. His efforts being generally appreciated and loudly praised. Joe R and I needing a few extra minutes to recover a normal breathing rate before we could join in to the tribute. Peace now being restored we went back to our party.

But not for long.

The enemy then made a near-fatal mistake. They attacked a superior force in a fortified position with insufficient assets. Perhaps a strategy session with the Sergeant Major could have been helpful.

Six FHBRD fags jumped on the roof of our lean-to pounding and screaming and cursing. A sneaky and cowardly attack, from behind, under the cover of darkness, and with bushes and shrubs to skulk off into if confronted.

Apparently, Phil was right, they weren't out of range of Bowie's BB barrage.

Joe R and I quickly rolled out of the lean-to. I was just as quick getting to my feet and hustling after our attackers. Joe was a little slower. I grabbed the first person I saw, a blond guy. He was a little bigger than me and hanging off the edge of the roof. Taking him by the arm, I spun him off the roof and into a bush by some trees about 20 feet or so to the right.

I then noticed I was alone.

I wasn't especially scared, but I was confused. It was very unusual for my friends to lose my back like this. So, after signaling to the attackers that there would be a momentary delay, I went back around to the front of the lean-to to investigate what could have happened for my friends to leave me alone like that. I found my comrades-in-arms huddled around Phil who was again holding his head.

"I'm okay, I'm okay."

"Enough with the beam already. Duck, would you Phil?" I said. "And, guys, its six against one out here! Could I get some help maybe?"

They sprung into action, all going around the left of the lean-to, behind Joe R. I walked back up the hill and saw five FHBRD fags conferring about 15 feet behind the lean-to, right on the edge of the shrubs, and escape. Idiots.

Wait a minute. Five? Where was the other one? The blond kid I tossed?

I located him. He was standing behind the bushes and trees on the right. About 25 feet from the now developing face off. What the…?

As I approached him, I noticed he was crouching in a pretty decent Bruce Lee, Karate style, fearsome looking stance. I laughed but he didn't seem to hear me.

I walked up next to him, unnoticed, and tapped him on his shoulder. Instantly, and with much altitude, he hopped around, always maintaining his Bruce Lee, Karate style, fearsome looking stance, landing full face in front of me, knuckles about 12 inches from my face.

"Careful, I know Karate!!" He declared, fulfilling his legal obligation to inform any possible combatant of his martial arts training.

"I can see that. But, wouldn't it work better if you could reach somebody? Isn't the fight, like, over there?" I asked.

As he thought this fact over, his crouch straightened up a bit, his arms relaxed a smidge, and his expression changed from fearsome to pensive with lines forming across his forehead. His focus slowly seemed to shift toward where my finger was pointing to the face-off between his friends and mine. He seemed frozen with confusion and indecision.

"Schmuck!" I thought.

"Hey I've got an idea. Why don't you and I go over there together and warn everyone about how you know Karate. And how they should be careful?" I suggested.

Apparently this seemed to solve his dilemma. He gave me a determined nod and pushed his way through the bushes and marched toward the escalating hostilities. I followed about

2 paces behind him, silently laughing and slowly shaking my head.

This is the scene I saw as I approached the confrontation behind the Blond Avenger.

Bobby, Joe R and Joey D were standing between Steve and the FHBRD fags by the corner of the lean-to. Apparently Steve emerged wielding the hatchet and they felt that that was a bit too extreme.

One of the FHBRD fags noticed the discussion.

"Hey, do you got a knife?" he demanded to know.

"If I had a knife, I'd stab you!" came the response from Joe R, who seemed uncharacteristically irritated by the interruption.

While this was going on, the four other FHBRD fags were face to face with Chris and Phil. And this argument was getting pretty fierce. The argument between Phil and Chris, that is. They were very busy fighting over who should hold the flashlight while the other kicks ass on the biggest of the FHBRD fags. Who was standing by patiently (maybe stupidly?) as Phil and Chris tried to solve their disagreement. The big fag was perfectly dressed for the stupid, er 'patient', part; cut-off dungaree shorts, black socks with red slip-on deck sneakers and the most hated part of the uniform for all casually dressed FHBRD fags, a tank top.

"Here, Chris, hold this. While I kick his ass." Started Phil while he gave Chris the flashlight.

"No, you hold it. I'm going to kick his ass." Said Chris, handing it back.

"Be careful I know Karate." Interceded our blond Bruce Lee, now about 10 feet from Chris. They ignored him.

Baton flashlight to Phil, "You hold it". Back to Chris, "No you hold it." "Be careful, I know Karate." Now about five feet away. Big FHBRD fag still waiting 'patiently'.

I thought this could have gone on forever. Phil and Chris could be very stubborn and the big FHBRD fag seemed to be extremely 'patient'. But the blond Bruce Lee really got things started.

He leaned in right over Chris' right elbow and screamed:

"I SAID, I KNOW KARATE. BE CAREFU......" He disappeared.

Chris, unable to ignore this insect any longer, turned and smacked the heel of his open right, and weaker, hand into his chest. Sending the blond Bruce Lee careening back about 25 feet, through some bushes, near some trees. Pretty much where I found him to begin with. That seemed about right.

But not to the big FHBRD fag. He finally got 'impatient'.

"Hey you can't do that to him!" he yelled at Chris.

Phil had the flashlight.

"No?!" screamed Chris. " I can do whatever I want to any of you!" He then started pointing. "I can kick his ass! His ass! His ass! And I can kick your ass! YOU AND YOUR FRIGGAN' TANK TOP!"

Chris then duplicated his open palm smash to the chest, this time sending the big FHBRD fag careening about 20 feet backward.

That seemed to break the stupid spell. They all, the 4 bystanders, blond Bruce Lee and the big FHBRD fag Beau Brummel, scattered into six different escape directions, all at breakneck speed.

We didn't pursue. We might have. We could have. We probably even should have. But I was never very good at pursuit when I was on my knees, struggling to breathe because I was laughing. And I was laughing very hard. Everyone but Chris was laughing just as hard as I was. I don't think I ever laughed that hard before or since.

It took us about 20 – 25 minutes to laugh ourselves out. In between fits, we got back to our sleeping accommodations, opened a new beer and put on a fresh Creedence tape. Every minute or two someone would lose control, start laughing, and the rest of us would be rendered useless for 30 seconds or so.

"Well, Bowie (bark), how do you feel about friggan' tank tops?"

"Well, I'm sure happy to be here".

But finally, we did calm down. So calm, that we actually got quiet. We could now hear the breeze in the leaves and the occasional chirp of a cricket. We all kind of settled into a calm that paralleled the peace emanating from our rare exposure to this pastoral setting. However, that was interrupted when a wailing voice arose from the lean-to to our left. The one containing our new honorary citizen from Flatbush.

"You, and your friggan' tank top!"

That shattered our every malaise and destroyed any chance for conversation for the next 15 minutes or so.

Just long enough for us to realize that if we were ever going to get the tank top out our system, we had to move the party down the road about 4 miles to the Blue Jay Inn, and its very entertaining owner, Frank. Frank was a displaced New Yorker who presided over this bar situated a couple of miles southeast of the Narrowsburg town center. The bar had cheap beer, a pool table, and a good jukebox. Frank was also a good bartender who could be relied on to keep the beer and drinks coming with a generous share of buybacks. He also kept the party upbeat by singing out his patented 'BEAU-TEE-FUL' chant every time he finished swallowing the last drop of his drink. All the bar patrons were expected to answer with the same chant and by draining their glasses.

I don't recall anything unusual occurring that night at the Blue Jay. Other than the newly sworn honorary Flatbusher introducing us to his five lean-to mates and the ensuing party we all had. We even got one of them to taste Frank's 'mustard', a very spicy homemade condiment based on horseradish, that he then made a lot hotter. Of course, Bobby won his typical $10 -$15 at pool. And, as usual, we were the last to leave.

The unusual waited for us to get back to the campsite, where we thought we lost Joey D.

Joey D was in Chris' car with Joe R and me and he was definitely feeling the effects of his alcohol consumption more than the rest of us. When Chris pulled into the same parking space we took earlier that evening, it was pitch black. With no moonlight and under the cover of very thickly branched trees you couldn't see your hand in front of your face. Chris left the doors open so we had a little light as we went to the trunk for flashlights. When we looked up, Joey D was gone. The three of us were shouting for him but got no answer. We agreed we hadn't heard a splash but we inspected the streambed anyway for any sign of him. We were getting worried he headed off back toward the highway, but we finally found a fresh footprint that led right onto the footbridge.

That same bridge that had taken him three minutes to cross in the gray dusk, took only three seconds in the pitch-black night. Obviously Joey D had developed a healthy dose of beer courage. We were joined by the occupants from Phil's car and hustled across the bridge fanning out in the hope that the six of us could cover the campsite fast enough to prevent him from injuring himself. Luckily, we had enough sense to send Bobby directly to the lean-to, where he found Joey D fast asleep and snoring softly in his sleeping bag.

The next day, Saturday, was to be canoe day, so just about everyone decided to settle down and get a little sleep. However, Joe R and I, neither of us wishing to end the day's festivities, decided the time was right for our ritual pre-dawn hike. We decided to try and reach the Delaware River by climbing over the hill behind us. It turned out to be a lot harder than we thought. We gave up just as the sun came up, maybe 90 minutes into our journey. The growing light allowed us of a clearer view of exactly where we were.

Which was lost.

Sort of. We still had a good idea where the road was, plus we agreed that the route had generally led us a bit west. We then just needed to find our way back to the road and head toward the sun. But which way was best to get back to the road?

That decision was made easier for us when we saw the beginning of a path that seemed to lead back toward Rte 97, albeit still a little more west than we wanted. We had had enough of rock walls and unyielding underbrush on the way there. So the prospect of a level, unobstructed route was very appealing even though it would increase the distance of our walk back. A short distance down the path we happily saw tire tracks. Definitely a path back to the road. Besides, since we didn't find the river, maybe this path would lead us to something almost as good.

It did.

The first thing it led to was frogs, or perhaps they were toads. I'm not sure. They were too small for us to tell. Less than an inch long. Thousands of them. Maybe hundreds of thousands. As the sun rose higher, they seemed to grow right out of the ground. Well, that would be because they did grow right out of the ground. They must have been youngsters, possibly even just hatching. The were so small and so numerous that it was impossible to walk without crushing a dozen or so with every step.

Skeevotz. So much for 'almost as good.'

With visions of 'B' Sci-fi Horror movies flashing in our heads, we ran as fast as we could to 'Escape from the Man-Eating Micro-Amphibians'. Well I ran, Joe did that thing we said reminded us of running. He had broken his hip twice when he was thirteen leaving one leg about an inch shorter than the other. Now as I have said, I'm pretty fast, but apparently the image of man-eating micro-amphibians must have made a deep impression on Joe, because he was no more than two steps behind me the whole time.

I guess you could say we were scared.

After about 75 yards, we were clear of the frogs. We took a few moments to catch our breath and laugh the fear out of our souls. Then, Joe R and I continued our hike down the now firm and frog-free dirt road.

But the 'B' Sc-fi Horror movie hadn't ended. Or, maybe this was a double feature.

Before we realized it, we found ourselves entering a small complex of about 6 – 8 long cabins, each two stories tall and arranged in a circle about 150 yards in diameter with a larger, three-story building in the center. All were made of wood with cedar shingle siding, and all had a single door, reached by a stoop of three steps, in the middle of the long side facing the center.

As Joe and I were passing between two of the cabins, a single, clear and loud stroke of a bell was heard. Not like a church bell. Not like the bell at a boxing match. Not like an oriental gong. But more like a combination of the three. It resonated like a church bell, had as little musical tone as a fight bell but it carried like the gong.

We stopped. Frozen in our tracks.

"Was that bell because of us? Maybe we stepped on a trip wire? Could they be mad that we trampled a few dozen of their sacred frogs?"

Seconds later, the entire complex started to wake up.

All the cabin doors opened simultaneously. A second or two later, out of the three story cabin in the center, strode a large, no, very large, black man in a pristine, shiny, flowing virgin-white robe. He almost glowed. He took about 4 steps from the door, stopped, and facing us, stretched his long arms out from his sides until they were level with his shoulders.

I wondered if it would be better to wave and greet the man, apologize for unintentionally trespassing and them wish him a nice day as we beat a quick exit.

Joe, reading my mind, grabbed my wrist. Shaking his head and putting a finger to his lips, he turned my attention to our left.

He had seen the line of people, led by a similarly sized man, also dressed in white robes, emerging from the cabin to our left. The 'central' large man then turned to face the door to our right, and a similar line emerged from there. He continued to turn in a circle, one cabin at a time. Watching as each came to life.

I guess you could say they came to life.

No one uttered a sound. No step creaked. No person coughed. No bird sang. No frog croaked. No cricket chirped. Just lines of zombie-like people marching single file out of their cabins. Eyes wide open, but no one taking notice of anything.

Not even us.

Especially not us.

Thankfully not us.

We very slowly and silently backed our way out beyond the outer walls of the cabin complex. We moved to our right and slowly, quietly - very quietly - made our way around the cabin to our right and headed back to get to the tree line so we could continue our journey to the road, without being seen. Each twig snap, each stumble, each rustle of leaves forced us to freeze in our tracks to make sure that that wouldn't be the sound that woke these people from their trance, identify us as infidels and bring them swarming down on us to sacrifice us to the man-eating microamphibians that they secretly worshiped, and we had inadvertedly defiled.

Thankfully we made good our escape. No pausing to catch our breath or laugh away our fears. This time we proceeded to the road, in silence, the only sound we heard was the tromping of our feet on the twigs and crisp leaves. Once on the road. We looked at each other and I ventured a weak overview of the morning's hike: "That was weird."

"Damn straight!" Was the best response Joe could up with.

Back at the camp, we climbed into our sleeping bags without any further comment. We never even told anyone about this.

We succeeded in getting a couple of hours sleep before everybody else woke up. Actually, it was me that woke up first, as usual.

"Hey, guys," I appealed, "if we're going canoeing we better get up and get going."

"Dope, can't you hear it's raining! Go back to sleep!"

"Oh? I didn't realize it's raining." I said as I climbed back into my sleeping bag. It was then I realized what made me a dope was that I was out from under the roof when they had convinced me it was raining. We all had mistaken the sound of the running water in the stream for rainfall.

I was disgusted with myself for being so stupid and decided to go for another walk, a shorter walk. I decided to getter a better look at the campgrounds. This turned out to be a good walk. I found the showers. There were six private wooden stalls situated westmost in the grounds and they even had hot water. I really wanted a shower, but with all the potential for mischief, it was something none of us would have taken advantage of if the others knew about it. So I quietly crept back to the lean-to for my bag with my towel and clean clothes. What a great feeling to relax in a hot shower. I did have to share the secret with the blond Bay Ridge guy who led the contingent of newest Flatbush citizens. The showers were behind his lean-to and when he heard the water he came to investigate. This remained our secret since there were no other insomniacs on the trip and we certainly weren't going to tell anyone else.

Cleaned, brushed, and dressed I headed back to find my friends struggling to get vertical. All except Joe R. He was snoring to beat the band.

After Joe R. finally woke up, we went to meet Charlie for breakfast. It was about a half-mile walk from the lean-to to Bob Landers, where the restaurant was, and where Charlie roughed it in a motel room. Besides meals and sleeping accommodations, Bob Landers was the canoe rental king in those parts. He had recently opened a new rental facility right at Skinner's Falls, the best part of the Delaware for canoeing. Previously, to go through the falls you would have to start about 3 hours north and navigate primarily boring water before the fun started. After the falls was another 2 hours of relative calm until arriving at Narrowsburg, where you could turn the canoes in. Now, we could start at Skinner's Falls and continue past to the Ten Mile River beach. This was right where we were staying making the trip a lot more fun and 2 hours shorter. This was good.

Our canoe trip started with the usual embarkation foolishness. Lot's of splashing. Some canoes overturned. A few inexperienced canoers going off in unintended directions. I was teamed with Phil. I wouldn't consider either of us inexperienced, but, after we shoved off, me in front and Phil in back steering, we couldn't shift out of reverse gear. Our canoe cut a lovely, smooth, graceful course that arced backwards into the river and continued upstream for about 50 yards until we ground back onto the bank.

I resurrected our previous argument about who should be in front and who in back.

"Get in the front Phil." I said as I climbed out of the canoe into knee-deep water.

"But…" he tried to argue.

"Get in the front, Phil." I cut him off.

He then tried to reason that this was his first time in back (I had always sat in back, albeit with different partners) and that he would get the hang of it soon enough.

"By that time we'll be in friggan' Ohio. Get in front, Phil." I countered. He relented.

The actual trip had some fun moments, though Phil and I stayed out of most of it.

"I don't want to get wet." Said Phil. "I'm getting a cold."

As he finished this sentence he turned to look over his shoulder at me.

"Spit! Look out!" He cried. Chris and Joey D were steaming up behind us so Chris could grab a hold of our canoe and rock it up and down until he got enough momentum going to turn us right over. Chris had us marked as his fifth victim canoe of the day.

Not to be.

Phil and I kicked in the warp engines and rifled out of Chris' reach, both of us being strong for our weight we could make the canoe fly. Chris now had to rely on a verbal salvo, but that got choked off by a large amount of Delaware River pouring over him as I scooped the follow-through of my strokes and drenched Chris pretty badly. Even Joey D had to laugh out loud at how soaked Chris got.

Next came the falls. Phil and I, plus every other canoe but one, got through okay. Joey D and Chris were the only pair of our group that swamped at the falls. Joey D., Mr. Scared-of-Bidges, at least when he is sober, had us all laughing when he yelled, "We're gonna die!!!" as he went into the water. I, and probably you also, would have taken a deep breath before going under instead of trying for the laughs.

Having solved our initial steering problems, Phil and I quickly turned to go help. Seeing Joey D. and Chris founder, neither can swim, we buried our paddles to fight the current to try and reach our friends. Actually, only Joey needed help. Chris had held onto the canoe with one hand and his paddle with the other. So while Joey was popping up and down in the rapids gasping for breath, Chris was riding along with the canoe. Phil and I were becoming impressed with the amount of headway we were making against the current, inching closer and closer to our troubled friend when a green canoe manned by two slender, tanned, bearded, hippie-types whizzed past us going upstream at about 20 knots (maritime phrase that means fast as hell) and got to Joey in a flash.

"Grab the gunwale, grab the gunwale!!!" (maritime phrase that means "hold onto the side of the boat") they yelled.

"What the... *gulp* is a....*gulp* flicking gunwale!!!" Screamed Joey (he obviously didn't speak maritime).

"Hold onto the side of the boat" they translated.

Oh,...*gulp* why didn't you say ...*gulp* so." Replied Joey.

Phil and I barely heard this exchange because we were now speeding downstream after having our wilderness egos trampled by the Grizzly Adams twins zooming past us to rescue our waterlogged friend. Who, since they had worked out their language barriers, were now conversing casually about appropriate social issues such as the weather, soap operas and whether Joey needed to be concerned about water snakes since he was still up to his chest in Delaware River. Actually, they were only kidding about the snakes.

Chris, wearing his unbelievably dry hat, continued to casually float downstream until his feet touched bottom. He waited there for the Grizzly Twins to beach Joey and reunite our least Olympic eligible canoe team.

The rest of the three hours included a large water splashing fight. The FHBRD fags lost that too. Chris' hat's dryness also survived the splashing. Incredibly, it actually made it all the way through the 15-mile trip, minus about 6 feet, dry as a bone. We all couldn't permit Chris to constantly remind us that his hat was still dry all night, as he had about twenty times during the post-rapids portion of the trip. By unanimous, silent poll, none abstaining, I was convinced to throw it into the water.

The next day we decided to do laundry. While our clothes were drying, Phil, Joe R, Joey D. and I decided to take a small side trip to Ft. Delaware, overlooking the bend in the river at Narrowsburg. Phil was now in a picture-taking mood so he convinced us that if we all bought $0.79 Tricorn hats and lined up next to the fence with the fort on our left and the river to our right, it would be a great picture. I don't think any of us agreed it would be a great picture; we just didn't have the energy to argue. So we followed along.

Hats on. Film in. Camera on post aimed and focused. Timer set. Phil hustles to position. Everyone all smiles. And then nothing. We relax. Actually, given the exertion needed to smile, the lack of sleep and excess partying, it was more like a collapse. Still in pose positions.

Click.

It is actually a great picture. Coupled with the successful one following we could probably sell them as a great before-after ad for Geritol.

The ride home was, as you might expect, quiet and very sleepy. Our moods were understandably quiet from all the fun and parties. We did waste enough energy to agree that a highlight of this trip was hooking up with the six Bay Ridgers in that lean-to to our left. They were a good find. It always felt good when you could include some new people in your fun. Tank top, the Blond Avenger, and the others who attacked our camp missed out because not only did we shun them but so did our new friends. We won that confrontation the best way you can, by increasing the circle we were partying in.

Even with this discussion, we mostly dozed quietly or sleepily gazed off at the wonderful scenery as we rode down Rte 97 and toward New York and home.

But we did get one moment of excitement. At lunch at Homers in Port Jervis, Phil remembered that his brother Tommy had invited us to spend a weekend this summer at his house in the Hamptons.

We picked up real fast after that.

THE SUMMER
OF '74 — PART II

As I have mentioned earlier, Phil's brother Tommy was one of the real popular guys in our neighborhood. His million dollar-smile and roaring laugh were a frequent occurrence and extremely infectious and he got a big kick out of the silly things we were capable of doing. So we got a healthy helping of Tommy as our audience. Plus, his closest friends also found us pretty amusing. So his invitation to hang out with him and his friends in the party-rich Hamptons really had our juices flowing. It turned out that only one of Tommy's friends would be there with us, and that was Russ. Russ was an intelligent guy who could be relied on to pay frequent compliments and offer comforting companionship. He would attend the parties but would usually stand aside when the craziness got into full gear. He was similar in a lot of ways to Joey D.

The trip to the Hamptons was scheduled for the second weekend in July. And, as has been happening fairly regularly, we were provided with our running gag for the weekend on the morning of the Fourth of July.

Phil stumbled out of bed that that morning and dragged himself upstairs from his basement bedroom/studio. His parents and a few brothers had just sat down to watch the movie '1776' on TV. A musical that starts with a song whose chorus demands that the obnoxious, boring, and unfunny John Adams "sit down, John, sit down, John, for God's sake John, sit down!"

Liberally applying this technique whenever we wanted one of our crew to stop something that was considered obnoxious, boring, or unfunny, we would all start chanting, "Sit down, Steve! (It was usually Steve) Sit down, Steve! For God's sake, Steve, sit down!"

Also, this trip took on added significance when we were very happily surprised that Steve had got in touch with Danny who was going to meet us out there. We had not seen Danny a lot since he moved out to Mattituck with his parents about two years before this trip. Danny had told Steve that he was going into the Navy at the end of the summer so our enthusiasm was raised even higher with the added incentive of giving Danny a proper sendoff.

We left on Friday evening at about 7:30 and arrived at Tommy's cabin after about a three hour trip. The cabin they rented was a small two-bedroom ranch house with a bare bones kitchen and bare bones furniture. It was situated at the end of a dirt road that ran for about 100 yards off the road that led to the beach. We didn't really take the time to get a thorough appraisal of the house because the party was waiting.

No unpacking. No settling sleeping assignments. We just dropped our packs and went out to the bars.

First stop was the Bawdy Barn. A great party place. Huge bar inside. Huge bar out back under a huge tent. But to enter we had to pay a cover charge. This was a new concept to us, but we happily coughed up the $2 apiece and filed in.

Danny was already there, his ride from Mattituck taking about a half hour. Tommy and Russ trailing along with an odd sensation that they might need to chaperone us. Tommy told Russ that his impressions of us were incomplete and he should expect practically anything from us, especially fun. He got his first taste very quickly.

Our indoctrination into the 'Barn' went so smoothly and easily it was no time at all before we felt as comfortable as the regulars. Our fun ran mostly along traditional lines: Chris' lips, Phil's thriftiness, my inability to live longer than 7 seconds without saying something. All our typical energy enhanced by Danny's presence. All was good with the world. All of us back together again, having fun, and we're at the Hamptons! Party city. The only thing missing was some music.

As soon as we noticed this, the band started to play, a Beach Boys cover band.

We moved to the left side of the stage and watched the band through a series of vertical wooden poles. The poles were about two feet apart on top of a waist high wall that separated the stage from the corridor to the restrooms and the exit. This was a great vantage point that gave us an excellent view of the dance floor and unobstructed access to the bar and restrooms.

The band was pretty good. They concentrated on cover songs of the Beach Boys but added in some other 'California Surf' music too. Not being much of a Beach Boys fan, I only like "Sloop John B" and "Good Vibrations," my friends enjoyed them more than I did. So I was concentrating more on the other people there than the band. My attention was drawn to an obviously obnoxious, bespectacled blond guy on the other side of the stage. He had on clothes that resembled the matching blue suits the band was wearing but he had a tie on instead of a vest. I believed him to be obnoxious because he was giving hand signals and direction to the drummer, singers and the musicians as they were playing. "If he's in the band, why isn't he onstage?" I thought to myself.

After about 5 songs, I found out why.

He focused a real nasty scowl at the lead singer and then looked at his watch. This must have been the cue for the singer to end the current song and deliver a glowing, enthusiastic, ass-kissing introduction for God's gift to the Hamptons partying world, 'Mr. Overdressed Obnoxious!'

He was welcomed by a warm round of applause, at least from the dancers in front of the stage. The audience of ten Flatbush immigrants standing stage left wasn't all that impressed.

They started in with his signature song, "Sloop John B," the band hitting the intro notes real well. I was happy because they were finally playing a song that I liked, and they were doing it real well. Mr. Overdressed Obnoxious sauntered up to the microphone and started to sing.

He sucked. Big time!

Our reaction to his desecration of his band mates' performance was destined to have an affect on the Bawdy Barn procedures, an impact that affects their patrons to this very day. Back then when you ordered a bottle of beer with a twist-off cap, you got it with the cap on. This turned out to be a regretful development for Mr. Overdressed Obnoxious. We shot off three rounds of bottle caps at the horrible lead singer who was ruining an otherwise fine version of one of our favorite party songs.

What do I mean three rounds? Well, you see, we're not the type of people to just throw bottle caps at someone. Anyone can do that. We organized our attack. Awaiting orders from our artillery commander, Phil, to launch simultaneous salvos at the intended target. Constantly adjusting for wind, altitude, and velocity before firing for affect.

"We come on the sloop John B." CLICK, CLICK, CLICK.

"My Grandfather and me." CLICK, CLICK, CLICK.

"Around Nassau town we did roam." CLICK, CLICK, CLICK, CLICK, CLICK, CLICK.

Our fourth volley was interrupted by a team of extremely polite bouncers who were very understanding of our displeasure with the lead singer. But rules are rules and would we be so kind as to leave. We returned this gentlemanly handling of our ejection by gentlemanly thanking them for their hospitality and headed for the door.

All of us except Steve.

He decided that some discussion with the bouncers would allow us to stay. He was wrong and he regretted it for the rest of the night.

As I was leaving, first again, I held the door for two couples to proceed me on the line to leave. The ladies were very kind and said thank you with big smiles. Their boyfriends were in front of them and holding out the back of their hands to a bouncer sitting on a stool, who stamped them with the word 'FRI'.

"What's that for?" I asked.

"So you can get back in tonight without paying again." Said one of the smiling young ladies.

"Cool!" I replied. Turning to Joey D behind me I said "If you get your hand stamped you can get back in tonight without paying."

"Cool!" Joey D replied. He passed it on. Every one of us, after agreeing that this was a 'cool' concept, got our hands stamped.

All of us except Steve.

Steve was being escorted out by one of the gentleman bouncers with whom he was so deeply engaged in a philosophical defense of our bottle cap indiscretion. Steve's contention was that we were right to show our displeasure like that because the rest of the band was real good and the idiot was ruining it for everyone. Besides, we are all endowed with a Constitutionally protected right of Free Speech. Or something like that. Of course the bouncer was having none of it.

When Steve caught up to us and noticed our stamps he also decided that it was 'cool and went back for his.

"Whoa there big fella!" Said the gentleman bouncer. "We don't stamp anyone who's being thrown out."

Now Steve got a little more excited. He started decrying loudly about the injustice of singling him out. More Constitutional quotes. More philosophical entreaties.

"Sit down, Steve. Sit down, Steve. For God's sake Steve, sit down!" This chorus echoed from Steve's six impatient companions not for the first, nor the last, time that weekend.

Our singing, and the bouncers' laughter broke Steve's concentration and his momentum, after which we succeeded in getting him to join us in our cars. Tommy and especially Russ showing great patience and amusement at the display we were putting on. We were now ready to head down the road to the next bar.

This was a down and dirty hard rocker place. Half of us got in before one of the bouncers asked for someone's proof of age, I think it was Chris. We got thrown out of there too when Chris protested a little too vehemently, getting into the bouncer's face and forcing Tommy and Russ to intervene. They were a little less amused here, not only at us but also at the bouncers who were a little more impolite than at the Bawdy Barn.

Moving on we came to Brendan's, the only disco out here at the time. But this was no ordinary Disco: it was an underground disco. It had a castle design entrance and plush carpeting in the foyer and down the stairway to the bar/dance floor. Very classy.

The social ramifications of us entering a disco cannot be over emphasized. Discos were in Bay Ridge and Fort Hamilton. Frequented by floral design silk shirted FHBRD fags who wore the shirts open to the navel and festooned themselves with a lot of gold chains. Not a typical place for 'regular' guys from Flatbush.

We all felt that we needed to do something special to commemorate such an auspicious occasion. So we rolled down the stairs. Rolled right across the dance floor and right up to the bar. I have to give them a lot of credit for their patience with us. We were allowed to have a beer or two before they asked us to leave, being almost as polite as at the Bawdy Barn.

There were two more bars on this stretch of the westbound Montauk Highway. Two more polite ejections. We then started to backtrack. Making a beeline for the Bawdy Barn again, since they were the nicest 'ejectors.'

All of us got back in without a problem.

All of us except Steve.

"Two dollars, please." Said the bouncer.

"But I'm with them. I coming back from before." Steve complained.

"Sorry. You need a stamp or you pay two dollars. Which is it?" Responded another polite bouncer. Steve again started to resort to philosophical and constitutional arguments to convince the accommodatingly patient bouncer that he could put aside the rules for Steve.

In the meantime, we had all gotten a beer and went out to the adjoining porch to see what Steve was up to this time. He was still busy decrying more injustice and arguing a foul on the part of the bouncer. Drawing a pretty sizable crowd to watch him lose again.

"Sit down, Steve. Sit down, Steve. For God's sake Steve, sit down!"

Our encore performance was thoroughly enjoyed by the onlookers but it caused us to be losers too, because it reminded the bouncers that we also had been ejected earlier and that we would have to leave again, being as polite as before. Actually they were more polite because they let us finish our beers before escorting us out. The bouncers took this delay to commiserate with Tommy and Russ over their immense chaperone responsibilities.

We spent a few minutes at Shooters and The USA Café, side-by-side bars about 1 mile east. Each time we again were politely asked to leave after 1 beer. And each time we politely complied.

Tommy suggested we try the three bars down by the beach. We then piled into the three cars for the twenty-minute caravan to the beach bars, Chris, Danny and Russ driving. There was practically no traffic at this time, maybe 2am, so our trip was quick, and without incident.

First stop was the Tiana Beach Club. I don't remember anything happening here but sometime during the third round we were again asked to leave, politely.

Undismayed, we strode into the Mimosa Club, next door. Mimosa had an odd age requirement for entry. In New York State the legal drinking age was 18. In Mimosa, it was raised to 23. For men. Women were okay if they were 18. But we had to have proof for 23.

Since the place was empty, the bartender elected to overlook this procedure and delivered us all a round of beers. When we asked for a second the owner appeared and, politely, reminded the bartender of his age requirement. The underage drinkers, representing 80% of his patronage at that time would have to leave. The bartender administering this rule reluctantly and with an apology.

The Hamptons was a real polite place!

The question was then raised, by a worn down Russ, "Should we call it a night and head back?"

"There's another bar across the street!" We replied.

To Russ' dismay, most of us started to walk across the street. The drivers drove their cars over to the parking lot there. Judging by the number of cars in the lot, this place seemed to be more crowded than either Tiana or Mimosa. It was just about now when the weather turned and a slight mist started rolling in.

I can't remember the name of this place but we were at our happiest when we entered and saw the reason for the larger crowd. They had some live entertainment that night and we nearly jumped out of our shoes when we saw who it was. Harry!!

Our burst of renewed energy and excitement was not welcomed by the other patrons or the bartenders here.

"Harry!! Allright!! Harry! Harry! Harry!" We started chanting as our first round was being delivered by a tired looking bartender. But the crowd looked as if we woke them out of a deep sleep.

"Hey Harry, play 'Taxi.'"

"No, 'Sympathy for the Devil'."

"Maybe 'Runaround Sue'."

We were bombarding Harry with requests of his best party songs we knew from hanging out at Michael's. Harry was a celebrity. Harry knew how to get a party going. Harry could do it.

But Harry didn't want to do it.

Harry was on his last song.

The round we had was last call. The general consensus was that they didn't need 7 asshole 18 year-olds crashing in at 3:30 in the morning and start screaming. But Harry understood that the best way to handle us was to sacrifice another fifteen minutes and play a couple of more songs, shut us up, and we would go away happy.

His last encore done, half of us with beers, half without, left us with a dilemma. What now? The bouncer, unpolitely, asked the four of us without beers to discontinue our pinball game and wait outside for our friends to finish up. We weren't altogether happy about this, but we left.

Outside things were worse than we expected. The mist had intensified into a steadier rainfall and that didn't help our mood much. Neither did the bouncer being unsympathetic when we tried to come back in to escape the weather, which we thought would have been the decent thing to do. But this bouncer wasn't decent. He wasn't very bright, either.

Finding ourselves out in the rain and denied the shelter of the bar, we climbed onto one of the round redwood picnic tables on the deck opening the umbrella for shelter. We four sat back-to-back, with me facing the door to await the slower drinking half of our crew. Suddenly, the bouncer came storming out of the bar and into my face.

"What are you doing?" He screamed. "You can't open that umbrella, can't you see it's raining?!"

This Steve-esque attempt at logic dumbfounded my three friends, but not me.

"Er, you may find this funny," I said with mock laughter. "But where we come from, people actually get under umbrellas to get out of the rain. Nifty idea, huh?"

He exploded. "Get off the table! Close the umbrella! Get off the deck! We're closed!"

Joe R asked. "A might touchy, isn't he?"

"He seems very tense." I answered.

"Everything okay at home?" Danny asked him.

"Get the frig off the deck!"

"Okay. We're going. But, would it be okay if I used the men's room real quick?" I asked.

"NO!" he called over his shoulder as he stomped back into the bar.

Now we were out in the rain. Left without beer, friends, music, or an umbrella. And now, no men's room. We resigned ourselves to the fact that we would have to find a way to persevere.

The three of us who had to go lined up next to the deck on the furthest side from the door and relieved ourselves. I was the only one still at it when our bouncer reemerged. And again he had a problem.

"What are you doing?!" He yelled.

"I'm off the deck." I said.

"No, that?"

"Oh, this?" I leaned a little bit toward him as if to tell him a secret. "This is called 'taking a piss'. You do it when you drink beer. Most people prefer to do it in a men's room. But, when there's none available, men can go off into the bushes to do it." Came my sarcastic, Kindergarten teacher explanation.

"You can't go there!"

My three friends chimed in, "When you gotta go, you gotta go."

The bouncer turned on them red with rage, tensing himself as if to charge at them. But he was interupted by the parade of people leaving the bar.

"All ready?" Tommy asked. "Good night." He said to completely disarm the flustered bouncer, wearing that million-dollar smile of his.

We piled into the cars. Tommy with Russ, who quickly drove off. Joey D and Steve with Chris. Joe R, Phil, Phil's cousin and I with Danny. Danny, whose car was a souped-up Olds 442, tore out of the parking lot to try and keep up with Russ because we weren't sure where the house was. Chris, who drove like his car was souped-up, tried to keep up with Danny. But the Chevelle he drove didn't have enough power to stay with Danny. As we roared down Dune Road to try and catch Russ, I looked back and noticed there were no headlights showing behind us. Danny got to the turn for the bridge very quickly and sped over into the fog and mist that was thickening as we drove east.

But this presented a bit of a problem for Chris. He had lost site of Danny's taillights as we sped off. He missed the turn for the bridge twice, once east bound, once west bound. Steve, Joey D and Chris realized that the turn must be back east and turned into a narrow dirt lane that led into the sand dunes on the ocean side of the island we were on. Chris misjudged the road and bogged down in some deep sand as he tried to turn around. They were struggling, trying to push the car free when they heard a strange sound.

Joey D's description of the sound needs to be heard, not read. But I'll try to give you an idea of what they heard.

First, think Doppler Affect. That classic recording of a roaring race car approaching and then the pitch of that roar suddenly changes to a lower note as the sound waves instantly shift from preceding the vehicle to trailing it.

Next, imagine that a few seconds before you hear that switch in tone, that the roar of the speeding racecar is drowned out by the sound of brokers and traders on the floor of the stock exchange on October 29th, 1929, as everyone is frantically trying to sell, sell, sell.

Putting this together: "ROAR, ROAR, ROAR, SELL, SELL, ROAR, ROAR."

Well, work on it.

What they heard was Danny's car.

After Danny made the turn to go over the bridge, our laughing and singing turned into a furious debate about going back for Chris, Joey D, and Steve.

"I don't see his headlights."

"Does he even know where he's going?"

"He'll be fine."

"I still don't see his headlights."

Danny was becoming distracted with the discussion and disturbed about what to do. He kept repeating, louder and louder as we descended the down slope of the bridge, "Do I go back or not? Do I go back or not?"

Then outside forces conspired to solve all problems, answer all questions, and settle all disputes.

The combination of his split concentration - music, debate, driving – and the speed he was going, Danny was unable to negotiate the hard left turn the road took at the bottom of the bridge. On any other day, he would have had no problem but that night the wet, sandy road was the final ingredient that did him in. The car started spinning counter clock-wise through the shoulder and across the lawn outside the Coast Guard station. Danny frantically turning the wheel and working the pedals trying to bring the hurtling beast under control. The car finally stopped, settling in the tall reeds on the other side of the lawn.

Did his passengers marvel at his heroic efforts? Were they foisting Danny with praise and triumph for saving their lives? Were they screaming adoring accolades at his skill and coolness under pressure? Were they overcome with terror and screeching madly as they clawed at the windows and doors of the careening juggernaut?

Not hardly.

"Straighten the car, Dan. Straighten the car, Dan. For God's sake, Danny, straighten the car."

"What are you guys friggan crazy?!!!" Danny screamed after the car lurched to a halt. After a second to catch his breath, Danny got a little hysterical. "I'm going nuts trying to save our lives!

And you guys are friggan' screwin' around! Music blaring! Spinning through the friggan' weeds! And you friggan' assholes! Go back for Chris! Don't go back for Chris! Go back for Chris! Don't go back for Chris!"

Phil, in a rare moment of empathy and tact, nodding at everyone reassuringly, found the exact words to sooth Danny's nerves, calm his frustrations and put everyone at ease. "Well, since we're facing that way, why don't we go back for Chris?"

"AAARRRGGGGHHHHH!!!!!" Danny screamed as he restarted the stalled car and put it in gear for the return trip over the bridge and, hopefully, to find Chris, Joey D, and Steve, who, though struggling with a bogged down car on a rainy night, were not too overwrought with frustration, that they couldn't appreciate how funny we sounded roaring and screaming by them three times before Joey D could struggle to the road to flag us down. Our contribution of extra arms and legs did indeed succeed in freeing Chris' car from the sand. We then proceeded without further adventure, and only a momentary misdirection, to Tommy's cabin to stake out the sleeping arrangements.

Mine was a chair with an ottoman. Phil and his cousin got one of the bedrooms. Chris and Joey D landed on separate sofas. Steve and Joe R on the floor somewhere. Danny decided he would be better off making the 25 minute drive back to Mattituck and sleep in his own bed. A good idea because nobody got much sleep as we relived the night's events before drifting off at about dawn. But not before Steve forced us to sing 'sit down' to him one more time.

The cabin started coming back to life about noon the next day. Each of us was struggling to get vertical until Russ emerged bleary-eyed from his room and inadvertently provided a little incentive.

"What a bunch of germs!" He said as he saw how difficult it would be to navigate through the living room to get to the bathroom and kitchen beyond. Tommy followed this up with that great laugh of his. Joe R reached over and turned on the radio adding his horrible sing-a-long voice to a Creedence Clearwater song that coincidently was playing at that moment. The laughter and music woke Phil's cousin who left the bedroom door open behind him as he joined us. The open door became an invitation for the rest of us to creatively try to find a way to get Phil out of bed. What finally got him up were the beginning strains of the theme from the movie "Jaws" coming from the radio. In time to the music and dressed in a red hooded sweatshirt, hood up and pulled low over his forehead, Phil began to stalk each of us around the room in an energetic 'Groucho-like' posture.

Our spirits soared. Joe R went to the refrigerator and opened a beer. Steve lit up a cigarette. Jokes were made about Chris' lips, Phil's thriftiness and my inability to live 7 seconds without saying something. Steve was told to 'sit down' once more. Tommy was roaring with laughter. But poor Russ was slouched at the kitchen table, his shaking head cradled in his folded arms before him as he lamented: "No. There's no way. They can't do it to me again. Not another night like last night!"

"Don't worry Russ." Came Joe's consoling efforts from behind him. "We have the whole day AND night ahead of us."

We actually had more than that. We spent years out at the Hamptons. We stayed in contact with those five guys who celebrated the "Bracelets" incident with us. We even stayed friendly with some of those bouncers and bartenders who welcomed us and treated us with respect, even when they were asking us to leave. It seemed that the places we came to frequent in the ensuing years were the ones that had the polite bouncers that one night. The staff that handled our escapades with disdain and anger never saw us again. They seemed to want to exclude us, so we reciprocated and didn't include them or their employers in the dozens of annual parties, planned or otherwise, we held over the years.

Our community stayed separate from theirs.

EPILOGUE

THE END

The end came without fanfare, without a parade, without a testimonial. It came on a beautiful summer's morning. A morning like so many thousand others. A commute to the City for the unlucky. A trip to the beach for the idlers. A walk to the park with mom for the fun lovers. Or a mission to the store. Perhaps a relaxed cup of coffee on the stoop. For two of those people, one, who chose the store, the end would be a nightmare, for the other, who chose the stoop, it would be the end.

Each citizen, each family, of Flatbush was going on with their business as usual, out of touch with the evolution our neighborhood was going through. As with any evolution the changes and developments were subtle rather than intense. But the change was indeed at hand. And its sweeping, broadsword stroke would be felt for Flatbush as a whole by one family in particular. Shep, a uniquely trained white German Shepherd, had probably picked up the paper from the candy store earlier so that Marty Sr. could read the news with his coffee. Marty Jr. also took the newspaper and his coffee to the stoop, but about two hours after his father. Just another normal day starting out in its normal fashion and expected to end in the normal way. But this was not to be. The last word that could be used to describe this day would be normal.

The paper was probably read like most papers would be here, starting in the back with the sports section. How'd the Yankees do yesterday? The Mets? Then the lazy scanning of the less important crime and political facts and of course, lastly the ads. All of a sudden, Marty's attention was disturbed. Across the street two kids heisted an old lady's hand bag. Two black kids, acting like hyenas, descended on a helpless victim caught off guard by the safety of the bright mid-morning of a gloriously beautiful day. I don't remember if they roughed her up, or if they just picked the bag clean on a run-by. But run they did.

Marty reacted as anyone who had spent their first 22 years of life in a neighborhood that taught, expected, and even demanded, support, courage, justice and tolerance from its members.

He said to himself, "Not today. Not while I can help. No way!"

Marty jumped in his car and sped after them. The culprits turned right and ran down 38th street. One way - the wrong way. Marty had to haul it down 37th Street to get to the corner of Farragut Road and 38th Street before the two fugitives.

He did.

The first one of the thieves to arrive didn't have the bag. But Marty stopped him anyway. He had something to say to these kids who couldn't have been more then thirteen years old. He then turned his attention to the slow one who did have the pocketbook.

"Give me the bag, and you can go." He said. "I only want the lady's bag back. I won't cause you no trouble."

I can very easily envision Marty saying that. He was that kind of guy. But, more probably, he was a little pissed and he let them know it. I doubt he would rough up or hit anyone as young as they were, but I'm sure some harsh words were exchanged.

But the faster one, he had a different idea how to handle this. He just walked up behind Marty and shot him in the back of the head. Killed him outright. As nice as you please.

In the Flatbush that I, and Marty, grew up in, this whole event was inconceivable. We had trouble making sense of all this. First, you didn't steal an old lady's pocket book. A bubble gum maybe, but not someone's bag. Next, you never, as a thirteen-year old, defied a 22-year-old. Not when he's right and you're wrong. Also, when you did something wrong and you got nailed; you took it like a man.

But this KID shot Marty. With a real gun. Real bullets. Real death. All because Marty did what he was supposed to. What the neighborhood taught him. But that neighborhood wasn't perfect. It wasn't the same as when Marty and I were thirteen. It didn't reach this KID the way it had reached us. It couldn't.

Because it had died also. It had lost its power and its magic.

The philosophy Marty was following had been diluted by desertion. We were moving out. The people who made up the community of Flatbush Brooklyn were leaving their homes for nicer sections of New York City. To Marine Park. Canarsie. Midwood. And Bay Ridge. We went to live at Breezy Point, Belle Harbor and Rockaway in Queens. Even foreign climes such as New Jersey and Long Island received some of our transfused souls.

Those who were left behind couldn't cover everywhere. It had definitely eluded at least one house on Schenectady Avenue between Farragut and Foster that instead bred a thief and murderer.

I can't say if it died just before or at the same time as Marty. But it was there not long before. As I walked, slowly, down the center aisle of St. Vincent Ferrer Church, as part of a procession of grieving family and friends, behind the casket that Marty was to be buried in, I was struck by the significance of what we were pacing off. Our steps mirroring the voyage that started in a neighborhood that had a finite geographic location and ended at a vague cherished memory. The buildings, the streets and the shops; the people; the Flatbush that I had grown up in had become an intangible. It had become an ideal.

I had to turn for my walk home, my new home about a mile away, not my home just 3/4 of a block from the church that was, for that day, the portal of our emigration to the outlands of the world. Mine was the Canarsie section of Brooklyn beyond the no-man's land of the junkyards, railroad tracks, and the Brooklyn Terminal Markets. The sunlight shone differently on the rest of the world. I saw its intensity dim as I passed under the railroad trestle crossing Glenwood Rd at 46th St. I sensed the ground develop an unfamiliar uphill grade on a road that I had walked dozens of times before. My soul and heart would not allow me to look back during this journey. My mind was instead instructed to find something to bring out with me to guide me on my journeys abroad. Those journeys that would become the rest of my life. My home, Flatbush, had evolved into something other than what it had been for the past three generations.

No longer a place to live. Now Flatbush had become a way of life.

I felt a need to share these stories depicting this way of life because I look around me at a world that seems to have missed the point. A world that seems to need to reassess it actions, its motives, and its rewards. A world that needs to eliminate terrorism and ensure security. A world that needs to reduce greed and increase justice. One that needs the courage to do the right thing. That needs to eliminate bigotry and include more people in the mix. A world that needs to focus on the human interactions that make us great. A world that needs to remember that it is the celebrations we share that bind us together.

The world's diminishing resources are being hoarded by a smaller percentage of a growing population. Something has to give. Can't it be us? Can't we put the matches away and close the car door and go to Boney's? Can't each of us cover our neighbors' backs? Have the courage to seek out our best road to excellence? Seek out only our just rewards? Allow for differences? Cheering each other on to excellence?

I look on this book as my first step to doing exactly that. You're included too. Just chip into the pool, your $5.00 on the bar, or maybe just a dollar for the jukebox. Do your part to help yourself and your neighbors feel safe, courageous, justly rewarded and tolerant.

And make sure to remember to celebrate and include Including.

1998887

Made in the USA